The Elements of Japanese Design

Crests of the Imperial Family and Its Branches

John W. Dower

THE ELEMENTS OF JAPANESE DESIGN

A Handbook of Family Crests, Heraldry & Symbolism

with over 2,700 crests drawn by Kiyoshi Kawamoto

A Weatherhill Book

New York • WALKER/WEATHERHILL • *Tokyo*

A NOTE ON DECORATIONS. The crest that appears on the binding and half-title pages shows wood sorrel leaves with stylized sword blades. The endpaper designs were reproduced from ink-stick rubbings of family crests on Japanese gravestones, and depict (left to right) square "mesh," tree ideograph in a handle enclosure, and folding fans in a circle enclosure.

First edition, 1971

Published by JOHN WEATHERHILL, INC., of New York and Tokyo, with editorial offices at 7-6-13 Roppongi, Minato-ku, Tokyo 106. Distributed in the United States by WALKER AND COMPANY, 720 Fifth Avenue, New York City 10019. Copyright © 1971 by John Weatherhill, Inc.; all rights reserved. Printed in Japan.

LCC Card No. 73-139688   ISBN 0-8027-2447-7

for Yasuko

Contents

Preface

THE DESIGNS presented in this book are called *mon* or *monsho* in Japanese, and for the most part they are a by-product of war. Men first began to use them for identification on the battlefield around the end of the twelfth century, when war in Japan was a pedigreed affair, and from that time on such emblems became a small but routine part of survival in the midst of anarchy. Men whose identity was hidden by armor wore them to prevent their allies from attacking them by mistake, and also to ensure just recognition should they perform heroic deeds. Then, as centuries passed and the designs gathered lore and developed familial associations, the warriors formalized and categorized them, and wore them primarily to boast of their lineage. These designs became the heraldic emblems of Japan.

Numerous comparisons can be drawn between the heraldry of Europe and that of Japan, but in the end one great difference remains. Where European arms survive now mostly as history, the Japanese crests have endured as art. Before all else they stand on their quality of design. They speak for themselves, and the purpose of this book is to give Westerners the opportunity to appreciate them. This is an art book first and last, and a historical footnote only incidentally.

Yet the footnote is an interesting one, for in a sense the crests of Japan hold a unique mirror to their land. To trace the full development of Japanese heraldic design—from ancient beginnings in the patterns on textiles imported from China, through involvement with the cultures of the nobility, warriors, and townsmen as these classes successively came to flourish—is to follow closely the prevailing winds of Japanese experience from roughly the seventh to the nineteenth century. In the end, in a way which has no counterpart in Europe, this development came full circle. Begun as ornamentation by an aristocracy of birth, it passed through the fire of feudalism and war to conclude with a brilliant, fin de siècle burst of decorative innovation in the hands of an aristocracy of looks and talent—the courtesans and actors of the "floating world" of seventeenth- and eighteenth-century Japan. This circle is the subject of the first part of this book.

On other levels, the crests reveal a spectrum of Oriental myth and image, a strict canon of taste and value, and a good collection of war and other stories—the last of which is a mixture of truth, embellishment, and apocrypha, and perhaps closer to the spirit of the times because of that fact. Together these several dimensions give resonance, color, and a little more depth to our understanding of the Japan of premodern times. By their very nature, the heraldic designs of Japan were simultaneously intensely intimate items and products of broad cultural, social, and economic forces. As such, they offer a small link between the personal and impersonal, and illuminate aspects of Japanese experience often obscured in the historian's overview. Chapter 5 of the text addresses itself to this relationship between the individual and the larger currents of his environment. Together with the commentaries on each separate design motif which accompany the illustrations, this discussion also introduces much of the basic symbolism of Japanese design. To enhance the reference value of the commentaries, some information about the adoption of specific crests is repeated there from chapter 5.

Since this book is designed primarily for the general reader rather than for the scholar, at the publisher's urging I have departed from my usual practice in several regards: Japanese words are here romanized according to actual pronunciation, and macrons indicating long vowels have been omitted (except in the index), giving, for example, *rimbo* instead of *rinbō*. The names of all modern (post-1868) Japanese are given in Western style, with the surname last; those of premodern Japanese, in Japanese style, with the surname first.

My personal interest in *mon* began with their grace. I first encountered them while working as an editor and book designer with John Weatherhill, Inc., between 1963 and 1965. We used them occasionally as typographical designs, and it was in searching for the most appropriate forms that I first began the habit of turning over carefully the pages of catalogues of Japanese crests. Meredith Weatherby, Weatherhill's guiding hand, shared my appreciation of this genre of Japanese art, and somewhere along the line we hit upon the idea of making the whole range of *mon* available to the English-speaking audience.

I took on the task of sorting out and identifying the crests and writing up what they were and meant, because this promised to be a brief and pleasant diversion. It has remained a diversion, and fortunately a pleasant one, because the brevity side of the proposition fell through. The history of the *mon* proved longer and richer than anticipated, the anecdotes livelier, and the symbolism deeper. The introduction to this book, in fact, derives from a thoroughly footnoted essay of approximately twice the present length, which is what the research side of the project grew to at one point. Although footnotes have largely been omitted from the present text, the major references consulted for both text and commentaries are listed in the Bibliographic Notes.

The protracted course of preparing the text was sustained by the knowledge that, for the crests themselves, we had located a remarkable collection of original drawings of *mon*. This happened almost by chance. In checking out existing Japanese catalogues of crests, an inquiry concerning one (*Mon no Seika,* first issued in 1906) placed us in contact with Mr. Yoshihiro Kawamoto, who held the present rights to the work. Mr. Kawamoto is the head of a Kyoto family which has traditionally produced and sold books catering particularly to persons engaged in the design and dyeing of kimono. I met him at his home in the late spring of 1965, a week before returning to the United States, to explain Weatherhill's proposed project to him, and in the course of the conversation he had a large cardboard carton brought down to us from the attic. It contained original drawings of *mon* drafted by his grandfather decades earlier, Mr. Kawamoto explained, and had been intended for a book which never came about. He offered us the use of the collection for our own publication.

Kiyoshi Kawamoto died in 1933, and his drawings are an impressive find. Each crest is drawn individually on a card three and three-quarter inches square; the drawings themselves are exactly one-third of that size and done just as they appear in this book—that is, the motif itself is left white, and what is inked in is the black of the surrounding area. Each crest is drawn with precision and clearly required considerable time to complete. Thus it is all the more impressive to realize that the total number of crests in the Kawamoto collection is between six and seven thousand, well over twice the number actually reproduced in this book. I know of no other collection of Japanese *mon* which contains so many variations.

I myself have spent weeks sitting before tabletops that were covered with Kawamoto's drawings, or on floors, surrounded by his work—this simply to select from among a multiplicity of possible variations on a single motif, and then arrange and lay out the book. And so I have a blurred but convincing and sympathetic image of Kiyoshi Kawamoto, kneeling before a low table in his home in the kimono-making district of Kyoto almost a half century ago, carefully filling out his delicate drawings, devising variations of his own, and patiently keeping at his task day after day for what must have been very many years in all. All this to end up, then, like so many men's lifework, in an almost forgotten box in the attic. With a limited number of exceptions, the *mon* presented here in *The Elements of Japanese Design* are reproduced from Kawamoto's originals. It is a pleasure to bring them to light again.

Several persons have been involved in one or another aspect of the book in the course of its preparation. Professors Albert Craig, Edwin O. Reischauer, and Donald Shively, all of Harvard, have read the manuscript at various stages in its development, and I am grateful for their comments and suggestions. As with all of their projects, the staff of John Weatherhill, Inc., have seen the book through with patience and care and taste; for all of this, I wish to thank in particular Ronald Bell, Audie Bock, Ralph Friedrich, Takeshi Yamazaki, and a fine mentor, Meredith Weatherby.

And for assistance direct and indirect, as well as a very good stretch of patience, final thanks must go to my wife.

Part One: Introduction

The Full Flower of Japanese Heraldry

CHAPTER ONE

The Courtly Society
and the Roots of Heraldic Design

S UN. MOON. Blue Dragon. Peacock. Somber Warrior (a tortoise). White Tiger. Three-legged Crow. These, rather than the familiar chrysanthemum and paulownia, were the emblems of the early Japanese sovereigns. The ancient court history *Shoku Nihongi* describes their depiction on the banners of the emperor Mommu in the year 701, and as such they are the most explicit early examples of fixed designs used as a denotation of person and status in Japan. All are Chinese emblems of great antiquity, and together they carry a ponderous mythology which made the ruler the pivot of cosmic harmony.

Like the borrowed emblems of the throne, the roots of Japanese heraldry were also alien and patrician, brought to the islands from China during the flourishing of the splendid T'ang dynasty (618–907). During these centuries, the Chinese influence extended to virtually all aspects of Japanese society and culture, from government and religion down through the smallest details of design. Here, particularly among the patterns on court costumes imported from T'ang China, is where the aesthetic roots of Japanese heraldic design are to be found. This genesis is reflected in the Chinese ideograph used to signify crest in Japanese—*mon* 紋, which can be broken down as "thread" 糸 "markings" 文, or in other words, embroidery. These origins are suggestive, for they reveal that the first aesthetic conception of many basic elements of Japanese design lies not in the techniques possible with pen or brush, but rather in the techniques possible with thread.

The Chinese patterns used originally on formal court attire by the Japanese courtiers were collectively categorized as *yusoku monyo*. Now they have blended, imperceptibly, with the body of indigenous design that a later, less Sinified society created; and because they possess that restraint which is commonly associated with Japanese taste, it is easy to underestimate the great extent to which these early Chinese motifs pervade the corpus of traditional Japanese design. Diamond shapes, circular configurations of "heavenly bodies," and several of the basic enclosures of Japanese crests such as the hexagon and "melon" (*mokko*) are among the *yusoku monyo*, as well as a variety of stylized flowers including the chrysanthemum, paulownia, wisteria, gentian, peony, iris, and lotus. Nonrepresentative floral patterns such as the "China flower" (*karabana*) and "brocade flower" (*fusenryo*) also belong in this category. The stylized cloud formation, crane, phoenix, and lion are likewise Chinese motifs dating from this early period. All of the above were used by the Japanese court as early as the Nara period (704–84). When, some three to four centuries later, the court aristocrats actually began to adopt specific family emblems, it was largely to this great repository of Chinese textile design that they turned. Warriors ascendant later, succumbing to the elegant life, also tapped this source.

In 794 the Japanese capital was moved from Nara to Heian (present Kyoto), where the *yusoku monyo* remained in vogue and gradually came to be used also on everyday clothing and for the decoration of furnishings and household utensils. In the course of the long Heian period (794–1160), however, several other aesthetic realms were cultivated which also were to contribute to the devices and motifs of heraldic design. Esoteric Buddhism was one of these, with its occult ornamentation. The exalted cult of calligraphy was another. And by the end of the ninth century, the luster of the T'ang dynasty having grown tarnished, a dawning of racial self-awareness began to find expression in new forms of art in Japan. In painting this was signaled by the emergence of the native *Yamato-e* school, and in design uniquely Japanese motifs were developed for almost the first time since the pre- and protohistoric Yayoi culture, when simple representations of such things as water, insects, fish, birds, animals, people, and dwellings had been made. The nobility of the later Heian period also turned to nature for much of their decorative inspiration, this time with the sophistication born of long Chinese tutelage, and the designs they produced then are still among the most familiar and beloved of Japanese subjects: foliage, grasses, butterflies, pine, blossoms of the plum and cherry.

The courtier class was small. Even at the peak of Heian culture, around the turn of the millennium, it is estimated that less than one-tenth of one percent of the population belonged to the formal ranks of the court nobility. Most of these families were interwed. Almost everyone knew everyone else. Almost everyone who counted, in fact, was related in some way to the great house of Fujiwara. And so there was no pressing need to select a personal or family crest. Yet before their stature was diminished by the horsemen from the provinces, many of the aristocratic families of Kyoto did come to fix upon a specific emblem as a mark of identification.

What guided them in this was partly happenstance, partly pride and taste, and partly traffic congestion. The very exclusive and cohesive nature of Heian court society fostered a concentration upon detail and concern with deportment and personal effects which enlarged small items of design and decoration into matters of very large concern in the daily lives of the elite classes. Individual preferences were noted and commented upon, and gradually certain individuals and then families became known for favoring particular designs. Out of habit, or out of pride in pedigree and veneration of one's progenitors, succeeding generations sometimes chose to pre-

serve these tastes, and in this way a rudimentary kind of heraldic identification began to develop among the courtly class. Informal associations along this line become noticeable around the eleventh century, and when it actually became fashionable to select one mark as a formal crest, the choice for many of the nobility had already been considerably narrowed by past family usage.

One mundane by-product of the life of elegance contributed perhaps more than anything else to the adoption of family emblems by the Heian elite. That by-product was the traffic jams and parking problems caused by the ox-drawn carriages used to travel to and from the court or to attend special pageants and spectacles. At times as many as five hundred such vehicles reportedly clogged the main avenues of Heian, and the literature of the period recounts the snarls and "carriage brawls" which frequently arose out of this situation. From the latter half of the eleventh century, certain noble families began to mark their carriages with a single design, repeated over the entire vehicle, to make it easier to distinguish. Several works dating from near the end of the Heian period include fairly lengthy lists of the carriage emblems used by prominent court families, and most of these emblems are identical with the formal crests later borne by these lineages.

The apogee of Heian society coincided with the heady career of Fujiwara Michinaga, who became regent in 995 and remained the dominant figure of the land until his death in 1027. The gradual emergence of patterns and designs as a mark of family identification among the Heian aristocracy took place after this, and thus coincided with the years of ebb. It did not develop to completion within the Heian period, and to the extent that it did develop it was not of great importance to anyone's life. It was, by and large, a small flourish born of great attention concentrated on decoration and family solidarity. Unlike the crests which henceforth were to appear among the feudal class, it bore little relation to matters of larger concern, such as killing and being killed.

Still, the early emblems of the court nobility are of interest in several respects. Not only did they eventually become an integral and especially graceful part of the body of heraldic design which survives today, but in addition their development came to both affect and be affected by the emergence of family crests among the warrior class—and in this can be seen both a play of artistic influence and a larger suggestion of the subtle interactions between the cultures of the two classes. While the beginnings of family crests appeared among the courtly class far earlier than they did among the warriors, the culmination of this development came later, pushed to its logical conclusion by the heraldic practices which emerged, independently and for different reasons, among the feudal hierarchy. And, in turn, the warriors eventually yielded to the softer life and culture of the court. This trend was already apparent during the final years of the Kamakura period (1185–1333). It became manifest in 1336, when a more venal breed of feudal leaders moved the center of government back to Kyoto from its feudal headquarters at Kamakura. Then the cult of taste was given new life, courtier and warrior commingled, and the dress and with it the crests of the citified provincials became more elaborate —influenced openly even by those hoary relics from T'ang China, the *yusoku monyo*.

CHAPTER TWO

The Warrior Society
and the First Bloom of Heraldry

THE MARTIAL CLASS which emerged as Japan's real ruler in the twelfth century established a culture and way of life almost antithetical to the delicate pastimes of the courtiers. Nonetheless, there were similarities and counterpoints between the two classes. Just as the court aristocrat had concerned himself with rank and lineage, sumptuous dress, and expertise in the gentle arts, so the provincial warrior took pride in the stock from which he came, his glittering battle array, and his proficiency in the arts of death. The men on horseback who transferred the seat of government to Kamakura in 1194 were, in vanity and pedigree and often in actual bonds of blood, cousins of the courtier class. Although their roots, at least for several centuries past, lay outside the capital and in the soil, they were nonetheless an elite—haughty, brave, treacherous, and comparatively rich—and like the courtiers, their caste was closed by birth and represented only a fraction of the population of the land, probably never more than five or six percent at most. Until after 1870, only this court-and-warrior elite had the right to bear surnames, and thus they alone were eventually in a position to adopt a family crest.

Despite these similarities, the rise of heraldry among the warrior class was obviously conditioned by the harsher, disparate features of medieval Japan—by the practices of land tenure, vassalage, and war. And as the war chronicles of Japan reveal, the first great flowering of heraldry occurred in the century and a half which followed the demise of the courtly class. In the epic Gempei War (1180–85), the clash between the Mina-

moto (Genji) and Taira (Heike) which ushered in the feudal period, there was in fact no significant heraldic practice. Combatants were not great in number. Battles were scattered, and often formalistic—warriors frequently announced their lineage before engaging an adversary in combat. Only two sides contended for power at this time, and it was possible to keep track of who did what. Consequently the Taira organized their forces under plain banners of red and the Minamoto under white, and the use of crests as a mark of distinction by individuals or groups was a rare thing at this time.

This practice contrasts with the early decades of the fourteenth century. Then, according to the *Taiheiki,* a military saga of the time, single armies flew two hundred, even three hundred, family crests, and the banners on which these were displayed streamed in the breeze like dragons and serpents, like pampas grass before the autumn wind. Ashikaga Takauji (1305–58) was able to map his route to dictator at this time by examining the many different crests on flags discarded on the battlefield by the enemy. A loyalist supporter of the emperor Godaigo, beleaguered and short of men, succeeded in dissuading the enemy from attacking him by painting the crests of all the warriors of the vicinity on pieces of linen and flying them conspicuously, so that it appeared he was supported by a great host of men. And the emperor Godaigo himself, returning in naïve and temporary triumph to Kyoto in 1333, rode in the imperial phoenix carriage followed by the great lords of the provinces, each accompanied by several hundred retainers and each behind his

6

own banner. The uncluttered days of the white and red had been replaced by a confusing medley of crests belonging to individuals, families, and feudal groups, and heraldry had been established in Japan.

Such use of heraldic devices by the martial class began almost immediately after the Gempei War and first appeared most conspicuously on three particular items of battlefield equipment: standards or battle flags (*hata*), a foot or two wide and up to ten feet in length; cloth curtains (*tobari*) used to encircle and partition off a commander's encampment; and an elaborate garment (*hitatare*) made of brocade or glossed silk and worn beneath armor, visible at the sleeves and legs. From these beginnings, formal crests came to be universally used and generously applied to virtually all items of martial equipment. Several explanations have been advanced as to why this development took place.

According to some accounts, the first significant impetus to the use of heraldic markings by the warrior class derived from Yoritomo (1148–99), who was the chieftain of the victorious Minamoto clan and the person responsible for establishing the feudal government at Kamakura. Obsessed by a desire to assert by all means possible his own preeminence in the feudal hierarchy, at the peak of his career Yoritomo is believed to have decided to retain the plain white banner as a symbol unique to himself and his immediate descendants. While continuing to use this in later campaigns, he reputedly directed subordinates to mark their flags in different ways and even personally granted the use of certain favored designs to valorous retainers. One interesting transition appears to have taken place in this respect, for it is reported that after the Gempei War Yoritomo ordered certain of his lieutenants to distinguish their battle standards from his by attaching different objects to the flagpole, such as fans or cutout geometric shapes. Eventually these retainers dispensed with the actual device and simply painted its likeness on their flag, and some later maintained this design as a family mark.

Even greater than this concern for token eminence was a purely strategic consideration, for the scale of warfare expanded suddenly and greatly after the Gempei War. Yoritomo's mopping-up campaign in the northern provinces in 1189, the abortive uprising of the retired emperor

Gotoba in 1221 (the Jokyu Disturbance), the Mongol invasions of 1274 and 1281, and the treacherous civil strife with which the Kamakura period closed—all saw the marshaling of scores of thousands of men, forces incalculably larger than the swift bands which had waged the Gempei War. Command and battlefield organization required more varied insignia, and the predominant simplicity of the earliest warrior crests reflects the military concern which motivated their adoption; most were plain geometric forms and simple representational figures. The three-triangle emblem of the Hojo clan is an example of this, while the Ashikaga clan adopted parallel lines, and the Nitta clan a black bar in a circle. Crests depicted in the *Scroll of the Mongol Invasion,* a thirteenth-century pictorial account of battles, include parallel hawk's feathers and different configurations of diamond shapes. Even at this early date there were exceptions to this general restraint, however, and the *Scroll of the Mongol Invasion* also includes one of the most intricate of Japanese crests—a circle enclosing the traditionally auspicious symbols of the crane, tortoise, pine, bamboo, and plum blossom.

Time, death, and birth also played their role. In 1199 Yoritomo was thrown from a horse and killed, and through treacherous murders his direct line of descent was extinguished by 1219. To a considerable extent Yoritomo's control over the whole of Japan had rested upon the ethic of feudal loyalty writ large, and with the abrupt cutting off of his line, combined with the death of those who had actually participated in the war against the Taira, this structure of allegiance culminating in a single national figure was undermined. Succeeding generations of warriors were detached from the bond of having been comrades in arms in that storied campaign, and economic grievances complicated by a natural increase in the warrior population helped further a more localized focus of allegiance and identity. Several of the most famous crests displayed on battle flags and encampment curtains during this first stage of heraldry—most notably those of the Ashikaga, Nitta, and Miura clans—were in fact initially used as a common badge of identification by all followers of these regional lords, regardless of kinship ties, and it was not really until the late thirteenth or early fourteenth century that the associations of heraldry began to pass through a finer sieve which singled out more exclusively the smaller family unit.

Another and more subtle factor behind the popularity of crests, one also seen most fully blown in the Muromachi period (1336–1573), derived from the gradual resumption of relations between the Kyoto court and the warrior class. The warrior's battle attire had always revealed a taste for decoration, and his susceptibility to the more distilled aesthetics of the court was well apparent by the end of the Kamakura period, when armies in the field passed the nights with poetry contests, capping verses in the lull between decapitating foes. Increasing contact with the court obviously enhanced the warrior's interest in fashionable patterns and designs. This early stage of heraldry was one of great flux. Crests adopted were not always retained, and when retained were rarely used to the exclusion of all other marks; even when the system of family crests finally became set and formalized throughout the land, almost every family possessed several different emblems for use depending on the oc-

casion. And so, yielding to the attractions of the gracious life, a warrior might change to a new or more elaborate crest, or embellish the one he had hitherto used, or simply retain one crest for use on the battlefield and select another, more elegant one from among the court patterns to wear on social occasions. It also became a common practice among the warriors to adopt one of the purely decorative floral patterns used by the court and give it a martial connotation by introducing stylized sword blades alternating with the petals.

This influence on crests was reciprocal. With the Kemmu Restoration (1333–36) and the subsequent interval from 1336 to 1392 when adherents of Godaigo set up a rival imperial court at Yoshino (near Kyoto), the court aristocrats discarded their palanquins for horses, their ceremonial robes for armor, and went to war. A number of the family crests of the aristocracy were adopted at this time in compliance with the heraldic practices already initiated by the warrior class.

CHAPTER THREE

High Feudalism and the Flowering of Heraldic Practice

Bᵧ THE TIME of the Northern and Southern Courts (1336–92), the use of crests was so well established throughout Japan that the authors of the *Taiheiki* could describe the forces which made up an army just by listing the markings on their banners, confident that their audience would recognize to which local lord each crest belonged. Despite this proliferation, the heraldry of the land was far from settled in its final form. There were no laws and few conventions governing this practice (the first books devoted specifically to crests did not appear until the sixteenth century); and while many of the crests prominent at this time continued to be carried as family emblems through succeeding centuries, a great many more fell into disuse with the decline of their bearers' prosperity and were replaced by the new emblems of those whom the pendulum of fortune favored, sometimes for just a while. The basic patterns, the simplest customs of usage, had been set down in a little more than a century, within the Kamakura period, but the refinements and manipulations which the system had yet to undergo were to continue for approximately another four hundred years.

The extended length of this gestation was interwoven with the larger developments taking place in Japan during this same time, developments which themselves seem to have been agonizingly protracted. The centuries following the Kemmu Restoration were devoted largely to slaughter and treachery which never went far enough to bring about order, and the country was fragmented into small domains whose lords, later known as daimyo, came to exercise such auton-

omy within their local spheres that the Jesuits arriving in the sixteenth century wrote of them as kings. In the anarchy which racked Japan from the fourteenth through the sixteenth century, the rise and fall of men of power was so rapid that they became characterized as "sudden lords" (*niwaka* daimyo), and the period as a whole is commonly described by the phrase *gekokujo,* "the overturning of those on top by those below." Warfare and personal relationships became increasingly complex, and the content of heraldry was constantly devastated and replenished, a clouded mirror of the times, as feudal houses rose and fell.

What heraldry eventually became in Japan was a system of *kamon,* or family crests; that is, the the use of a distinctive mark as symbol of one's family name. The designation "family crest" in itself tells little, however, for the conception of the Japanese family changed drastically in the period of high feudalism. Despite the decimations of war, the population of the warrior class grew rapidly during the feudal period, and the traditional blood groupings of the Heian period —split from within by natural growth, broken down from without by social and economic change—slowly splintered into small units, often of a single household. This breakup of highborn families was accelerated from the fourteenth century on by the adoption of a rule of primogeniture for the inheritance of an estate—a procedure which forced younger sons to form independent families of their own, often adopting a new surname in the process. By the end of the feudal period the Minamoto clan, for example, subsumed 4 subclans, 27 major branches, and 569 different surnames, while families bearing some 696 different surnames claimed descent from the Fujiwara line, and another 206 surnames derived from the Taira. The immediate effect of this great social transformation upon the practice of heraldry was obvious. Crests which previously had served as the common emblems of large kinship groups were no longer adequate. New variations had to be devised to represent new name groups and newly independent families.

Because this splintering of families continued through several centuries of almost total chaos, when written documents were not the greatest of concerns and a family here today might well be gone tomorrow, and also because each family invariably adopted one or several "substitute crests" (*kaemon*) in addition to its formal mark (*jomon*), the picture of heraldry which emerges during most of this period is broken and incomplete, obscured by the dust of battlefields and the uncertainty of the family group. And yet, for all this, it attains great clarity on occasion as some keen warrior hacks his way to an eminence and unfurls his flag for all to see. Heraldry flourished, in part because of this very confusion of the family system, for this increased the importance of crests as a specific mark of identification and eventually firmed the heraldic system as a whole by making necessary the publication of books of crests and giving rise to certain conventions of usage.

While complicating heraldry, the breakup of families also immeasurably enriched it in the realm of pure design by demanding of the Japanese gift for composition an ever greater subtlety. Looking at these crests as a small side stream of Japanese art, one is struck not only by their fineness of conception, but also by the tremendous number of variations which are based on common motifs. Some might argue that this makes for tedium and reveals a dullness of imagination, and here and there it does. But there is also a deeper impression here, perhaps peculiarly Japanese: that of turning something over slowly in the eye of the mind, of finding an infinite variety and delight in the smallest and most familiar of things. In a manner similar to the conventions of Japanese poetry, once a body of standard forms had been established, there was

little inclination to range afield in a search for strikingly new motifs. If for some reason no one had used a fish before—and it seems curious that they did not—then no one used one later. As a result, the many new crests which continued to appear up through the sixteenth century tended to remain within the categories established during the early stages of feudalism, and families absolutely unrelated often came to bear emblems of close resemblance.

At the same time, the breakup of families gave a practical dimension to this adherence to traditional elements of design, for when new branches emerged to set up a semi-independent existence, it was to the advantage of some of them to display, as clearly as possible, the good wood of their stock. Thus many new families used, either as their main or secondary crest, an emblem which varied only slightly from that of their senior or more prestigious branch. A great many derivative families, however, appear to have deliberately adopted crests distinct from that retained by their parent line—an expression of independence, perhaps, and in some instances clearly a gesture of animosity.

There was also another side to the use of widely recognized motifs. Pedigree retained prestige in the period of high feudalism, but abstractly, in an ideal realm, denied that final awesomeness which previously had lent it weight in practical affairs. Not only was the authority of seniority and lineage compromised by raw power realities, but the very question of lineage itself—further complicated by adoption, intermarriage, illegitimate children, and the utter disorder of genealogical records—became so entangled that vassals newly risen from obscurity frequently assumed as part of their martial spoils the right to use a surname of renown or, in many cases, actually to claim descent from one of the "four great clans" (Fujiwara, Tachibana, Minamoto, and Taira). Thus lowborn men of real power also frequently grasped at vestiges of social status and respect by deliberately adopting an emblem closely resembling that associated with a great noble family or known to have been used by some true warrior-aristocrat of the past. In some cases the plunder was even more forthright, and several instances are recorded where family crests were appropriated directly from an enemy defeated in battle.

As derivative crests became more numerous, certain fixed conventions were created whereby variations of design might be made. These were simply conceived and exceptionally ingenious, a compendium of designers' wit, and a full listing of these devices would easily number more than a hundred. The most common method of alteration was the addition of an enclosure, either circular or rectilinear, and here alone there were developed some fifty or more conventionalized forms. Alternatively, a crest might be revised by introducing new elements to the established design itself; by simplifying it; by changing the style of drawing; or by altering the perspective from which a given motif was portrayed.

In many respects this practice resembled the way in which European crests were varied, but no matter what the manner of alteration might be, one basic rule was scrupulously observed which helped place the Japanese crests aesthetically on an entirely different plane from the devices of European heraldry. This was the rule of disparate elements, and these were anathema. Different objects might be combined in an emblem, but with few exceptions they were always intrinsically harmonious. Such discretion was made easier by the badgelike nature of Japanese crests and predominance of motifs derived from nature, but it also drew from a deeper wellspring of taste which precluded the possibility of such grotesqueries as the marshaling, impalement, and hard symbolisms European heraldry sometimes produced. Japanese crests were also usually rendered monochromatically, though the color might vary depending on the use and background, and this absence of fixed or variegated coloring eliminated from the start the development of any conventions of alteration which could be compared to those of Europe.

To set themselves apart in the midst of this profusion of heraldic designs, the warriors resorted to various means of identification which previously had not been used in Japan. Crests which originally had been displayed primarily on battle flags, encampment curtains, and the garment worn under the armor now became painted, embroidered, woven, lacquered, or worked in iron on almost every conceivable part of the warrior's equipment—scabbards and guards of swords and daggers; sheaths of spears and halberds; quivers; shields; saddles, stirrups, and

bits; helmets (between the ornamental "horns" and also on the rim); many parts of the armor (neck, shoulder, breast, back, arm, and hand pieces); cases in which armor was stored; clothing and equipment boxes; and on the paper lanterns used in a commander's encampment. Smaller flags (*kohata*), as well as a distinctive little pennant (*kasajirushi*) which was attached to the front or back of the helmet, came into use in the latter part of the Kamakura period to display heraldic emblems, and around the time of the Onin Civil War (1467–77) a streamer known as *nobori* or *hata-nobori* became especially popular; this was hung from a horizontal crossbar attached to the top of the flagpole so that the streamer might trail in the wind.

In the sixteenth century, when the entire country was disrupted by civil wars and the scope and techniques of warfare had vastly changed, a number of new articles of military equipment unfamiliar to the West were adopted and used, either primarily or incidentally, for heraldic purposes. Among these were the *umajirushi*, a pole topped by devices such as fans, tassels, and solid three-dimensional crests and carried by the side of the commander; *sashimono*, decorations of a similar type, attached to a rod and worn on armor, or attached to the top of a flagpole; *yarijirushi*, lances with crest-bearing pennants attached; and the *horo*, a baglike piece of cloth about five feet wide, sometimes given shape with bamboo bones, which was affixed to the front of the armor and brought forward over the horse's head as a protection against arrows. Within a short time after the Japanese first learned of firearms from the Portuguese in the 1540's, local manufacture of these was perfected and they were put to devastating use in the civil wars, with crests sometimes embossed on the muzzles of both muskets and cannons. Influenced by the clothing of the Portuguese and Spaniards, the warriors also later devised a long, sleeveless coat called the *jimbaori*, which was worn over armor but removed before actual fighting took place. Sometimes embellished with crests, embroidered or worked in gold, the *jimbaori* was the nearest approximation to the European coat of arms. On ships, crests were displayed on pennants and curtains and sometimes in gigantic size on sails.

This compulsion to make a striking display carried over to the fleeting interludes of peace as well, and during the period of high feudalism a variety of ostentatious costumes made their appearance among the lesser members of the warrior class. The most interesting of these insofar as heraldic design was concerned was the overpowering formal costume known as the *daimon,* or "great crest." This was a *hitatare* with huge billowing sleeves on which the wearer's family crest was reproduced in enormous size. Most familiar today in Kabuki prints, particularly those depicting the Danjuro line of actors, these crests were half as tall as a man, and quite distant from the professed austerity of the warrior's creed.

The disorder of the period of high feudalism made identification and recognition confusing but all the more essential, and in this setting heraldry became a small gesture toward stability, not only figuratively but in actual practice. One of the interesting aspects of the use of crests in this period, in fact, is the more political use to which they were put. Because this was an upstart, uncertain age, the very men who themselves broke tradition came to treasure all the more whatever visual symbols they might acquire which carried with them connotations of strength, endurance, and continuity—and perhaps even more, of legitimacy. Thus among the most esteemed crests were those conferred upon social inferiors by the imperial house or one of the Fujiwara families, or those bestowed upon a daimyo by the shogun (the military overlord of the land) or upon a vassal by his lord. At the same time, the transfer of crests among social equals as a symbolic seal not infrequently accompanied the political marriages and adoptions by which powerful families endeavored to stabilize their relations.

Perhaps the most interesting aspect of this transfer of crests was the granting of permission to use the imperial chrysanthemum and paulownia crests. Both of these motifs had been used privately by the imperial family from the beginning of the Kamakura period, placed on personal clothing, furnishings, and household utensils, and in the course of the early feudal period they gradually replaced the earlier symbols of the throne. The emperor Kameyama (reigned 1259–74) is reputed to have been the first to bestow the chrysanthemum crest upon a loyal subject, but it was the emperor Godaigo, some seventy years

later, who most conspicuously brought forth both emblems from the recesses of the imperial household and placed them before the public eye—displaying them on his banners and establishing them, in effect, as sovereign orders of merit. This practice of bestowal, followed erratically for the next several centuries, played an ironic role in the development of heraldry in Japan. While the introduction of the imperial emblems among the crests of the warriors gave undoubted prestige to heraldic display in general —until almost the end of the sixteenth century no crests were more prized than the chrysanthemum and paulownia—at the same time few men were subjected to greater indignities during this period than the emperors themselves. Their crests were better esteemed than their persons. Despite these abuses, however, their sovereignty in the abstract remained inviolate, and powerful warriors who themselves abused the throne coveted the throne's symbols nonetheless. Throughout the period of high feudalism and even into the Edo period (1600–1867), families upon whom the imperial crests had been bestowed displayed them with honor, and many who had not actually received them sought to pose as having done so by forging family records. In the closing decade of the sixteenth century it was actually found necessary to issue edicts expressly forbidding unauthorized use of the chrysanthemum and paulownia. These edicts proved abortive, and in later centuries both emblems came to be appropriated at will, eventually appearing as trademarks and patterns on commercial goods, and even as the crests of courtesans.

A similar dichotomy between the mundane and ideal was manifested in the prestige engendered by crests of the high court nobility long after this class had ceased to perform an important function in society. This was particularly true of crests belonging to the *gosekke,* the five main branches of the Fujiwara clan, who traditionally monopolized the position of *kampaku,* or regent to the emperor. Although these nobles were quite literally on the dole during much of the period of high feudalism, families who were granted permission to use their emblems gained considerable face thereby.

While the lofty place accorded by the warrior class to crests bestowed upon them by the throne and court nobility tells something of the impress which traditional hierarchic notions continued to make upon the feudal mind, the transfer of crests from warrior to warrior was more prevalent and more in keeping with the feudal ethos. Even this, however, had its ironies and involutions. On the highest level within the feudal structure, that of the shogun, the bestowal of crests was not practiced with any regularity until the time of Ashikaga Yoshimasa, whose term in office ran from 1443 to 1479. The crest used by Yoshimasa and his successors on such occasions, moreover, was not the formal parallel-line crest of the Ashikaga, but rather the paulownia crest which their progenitor, Takauji, had earlier received from the throne. With a perverse appropriateness, the century during which the Ashikaga shoguns used this emblem to honor (and firm up) the support of other lords coincided with the nadir of their own fortunes, for by the sixteenth century they had declined to being little more than pawns in the hands of certain lords. Yet here again the aura of legitimacy—in this case the legitimacy of the shogun's office—continued to hold magic even if those who actually held the office had none, and the crests thus bestowed were worn respectfully by daimyo who were themselves more powerful than the Ashikaga. After the demise of the Ashikaga in 1573, the most conspicuous conferral of crests at the apex of the feudal pyramid took place at the hands of Toyotomi Hideyoshi, who as the de facto ruler of Japan from 1582 to 1598 made the greatest single contribution to ending the period of civil war. Like the Ashikaga, Hideyoshi had received the paulownia crest from the throne. Unlike them, he used this in slightly altered form as his main family crest and permitted this same variation to be displayed by his most loyal retainers.

Lower down on the feudal scale, the conferral of crests which took place between individual daimyo and their retainers was a practical as well as a social honor, and frequently went hand in hand with priorities of rank and stipend. In several domains vassals granted the right to wear their lord's family crest were actually designated as a separate group and listed in the daimyo's family registers immediately following blood kin. In Japan as in Europe, such conferral actually manifested itself in some cases in a marked geographic concentration of common emblems.

Among the daimyo themselves, permission to use another lord's family crest often accompanied intermarriages and adoptions. The swallows-and-bamboo crest of the powerful Uesugi family of eastern Japan, for example, was involved in a number of complex transactions of this nature. Annals of the period also mention several occasions on which family crests were said to have been exchanged by daimyo simply as a sign of mutual respect and support. Despite the prevalence of such transferrals, however, the emblems involved in these relations almost always remained intact, and there developed no strong symbolic conventions comparable to the marshaling of European arms, whereby elements of different crests were combined to show such alliances.

There did not develop in Japan, either during the period of high feudalism or later, any formal body of rules concerning heraldry. The forms and conventions which guided the design and use of crests derived almost entirely from a long evolution of customary practice, and even in its final stages Japanese heraldry did not know a precise lexicon and code of usage such as that which was established in the West. This was probably predictable. The binding and leveling force of custom in traditional Japan can hardly be overestimated; its conservative role in the society was more pervasive by far than written law and legislation, and even if a more formal code of heraldic regulation had been deemed desirable, this was, during the centuries when heraldry saw its most rapid growth, a war-ravaged country which afforded neither the opportunity nor the neutral ground where men might meet over such a concern. By the Edo period, when peace was established by the Tokugawa shoguns, Japanese heraldry had, quite independently of such control, developed its own traditions—looser than those of Europe, but obviously satisfactory to those who were most concerned, the warriors and court aristocrats themselves.

The few general laws which did emerge were almost all prohibitions directed against the unauthorized use of particular crests, an abuse which the transfer of crests encouraged. The ineffective edicts against misuse of the imperial emblems were the best known of these regulations, and certain daimyo protected their own family crests by including similar stipulations in their house laws. In the eighteenth century even the dominant Tokugawa found it necessary to issue legislation restricting use of their hollyhock emblem, particularly after a certain *ronin* (masterless warrior) spent a large part of the year 1722 wearing this crest on his garments and swindling shopkeepers in Edo (present Tokyo). The prohibition which followed this incident included the interesting acknowledgment that "until now there have been many indiscretions involving the use of the hollyhock crest on garments. Men and women of the very lowest classes have been wearing this. . . ." The usurpation of the trappings of the privileged classes by the commoners, discussed more fully in the following section, had reached even into the shogun's closet by that time.

While crests were transferred with some freedom, and similarities of motif were common, there was at the same time a fine sense of encroachment. The daimyo Date Masamune demonstrated this with some vigor by executing one of his own retainers for wearing a crest similar to his own without authorization, and there were numerous instances in which persons temporarily or even permanently changed their crest to avoid giving offense to superiors whose family emblems happened to bear a resemblance to their own. This took place even well into the Edo period, when as a part of their policy of keeping potential rivals weak, the Tokugawa rulers reassigned daimyo to entirely different fiefs; warriors thus suddenly presented with a new lord might be obliged to change their crests, and even surnames, if these by chance coincided with his. In 1771 a hapless envoy from Choshu (now part of Yamaguchi Prefecture) was stripped of his garments upon entering Tosa (now Kochi Prefecture) because the crest he wore—his legitimate family crest—was identical with one of great prestige in that latter domain. Several years later this envoy's son paid a visit to Tosa, and on this occasion it was duly noted that he wore his family's substitute crest.

This custom of a single family possessing several different crests, especially when set against the more severe conventions of Europe, is one of the most striking features of Japanese heraldry and often cited by those who regard the Japanese development as undisciplined and unsophisti-

cated. By the seventeenth century there was scarcely a family among the upper classes who did not possess and regularly use several family crests. Among daimyo, for example, one Date family used seven family crests, one Yamanouchi family used nine, and the Kii branch of the Tokugawa used fourteen, although in this latter case the crests were almost all variations of the hollyhock design. The most compulsive collectors among vassal families were the Itami, who possessed thirteen family crests. These were, however, exceptional cases, and on the average a family regularly used only two or three different emblems.

One manner in which a family might come to acquire additional crests was, of course, the custom of transfer. Another lay in the enlargement of warfare to mass encounters and the use of individual marks this confusion provoked, for since the use of crests as a mark of identification evolved through a period of some four hundred years prior to the Tokugawa peace, there was ample opportunity for a family to become associated with a number of different crests, many of which were of good connotation and not likely to be discontinued. To this must be added also the element of pure visual delight. The earliest crests of the warrior class were for the most part severe and simple battlefield emblems, but as these marks came to stand for a family and be placed on everyday clothes, there clearly arose a desire for separate and more decorative emblems better suited to social use in the interludes between wars. Families in certain parts of Japan also came to make a distinction between the crests used by women and those used by men.

Because each family possessed several crests, and often favored one lately received over that first adopted or most frequently employed in the past, heraldic practice in Japan was more flexible than that of Europe and more subject to change of heart. But it was not mere disorder. It served its purpose adequately and gave aesthetic pleasure as well, and it was, moreover, subject to conventions of its own which actually brought it more in line with European practice than at first might appear. For practical purposes it was necessary that each family designate one of its crests as its main or official mark. This was most commonly called the *jomon* (established crest), or alternatively the *hommon* (main crest), *shomon* (genuine crest), *omote mon* (front crest), or, because it was this that was most often used in battle, the *buko no mon* (crest of martial merit). All other crests used by the family were designated most usually as *kaemon,* but also as *fukumon* (supplementary crest), *betsumon* (separate crest), *hikaemon* (reserve crest), or *uramon* (rear crest). It was the *jomon* (formal crest) that was of course most important, worn on official occasions, and listed as the family crest in genealogies and in the books of heraldry which appeared in the Edo period. When a daimyo bestowed his crest upon a favored vassal, it was almost invariably the *jomon* which he gave.

Many families retained as *jomon* the first crest which they had adopted early in the feudal period, but throughout the period of high feudalism there were frequent instances of *jomon* being changed, and it was not really until the first several decades of the Edo period, when warlords denied wars became in effect governors and bureaucrats, that the firm selection of a *jomon* actually became imperative. However, whether the final designation of one crest as official was postponed until that time or made earlier, this choice was usually determined by weighing against the crest longest possessed several other considerations, especially military merit and the prestige of crests received by transfer.

It was custom and convention too, more than minute rules, which eventually gave to crests a uniformity of style and taste. The earliest Japanese crests were often rough and crudely drawn, and some adopted later were eccentric and queer. Time brought refinement and eliminated the outlandish. Changing social needs and fashions of dress imposed requirements of size and symmetry, and considerations of weaving and later of dyeing brought with them further modifications of conception.

During the period of high feudalism the warriors adopted as their standard everyday apparel a garment known as the *suo,* which had originally been worn by commoners, and for formal occasions they wore a stiff, sleeveless robe known as *kataginu;* crests were displayed on both of these, and this exercised a restraining influence upon the design of these emblems which proved more enduring than the flamboyance of the previously mentioned *daimon,* or "great crest" costume. In the Edo period, the small-sleeved kimono known as *kosode* became the daily costume of both men and women, and the *haori,* a light, half-length coat, was popularized as a formal overgarment for it. The standardization of these garments, together with the conservative tone of official conduct in general, encouraged the final formalization of the design of crests. Symmetry, a characteristic of most crests from the very beginning, was even more consciously emphasized by placing an enclosure, usually circular, around almost all designs, while coloring, which had been used sparingly in the past, was dropped almost entirely. The placement of crests on garments also became conventionalized at this time in the "three places, five places" arrangement (on the back centered above the shoulder blades, on the sleeves by the shoulders, and occasionally— especially among the upper classes—high on the breasts). On formal wear, crests were generally rendered about an inch and a half in diameter.

At the same time, as crests became more firmly established as set marks of familial identification, the necessity of being able to reproduce them exactly became imperative, especially to scribes, dyers, and weavers, and as a result fixed rules of draftsmanship were developed, and a specialized vocabulary was created to describe the many possible styles of drawing and composition. This vocabulary is fairly precise, and suggests many correspondences to the technicalities of European blazonry.

CHAPTER FOUR

The Floating World and
the Full Circle of Heraldic Design

WITH TOKUGAWA Ieyasu's decisive victory at Sekigahara in 1600 and the establishment of the strong and conservative Tokugawa shogunate three years later, the feudal system was frozen as a rigid social and political structure which was to endure for some two and a half centuries of domestic peace. Warriors were denied their wars, and with this their traditional avenue of bettering their position. Battle flags, encampment curtains, armor—in fact most of the articles of war on which crests had originally been displayed—were put aside, and the martial arts themselves became athletic pastimes. Status was the cornerstone of this society, and it was as a conspicuous mark of status that crests were finally dignified and systematized during the first stages of Tokugawa rule. The full bloom of heraldic practice, however, contained within itself the seed of its own destruction.

The greatest single development contributing to both the formalization and disintegration of orthodox heraldry in the early Edo period was undoubtedly the *sankin kotai* system of alternate residence, whereby the various lords of the land were required to spend half of their time at Edo under the watchful eyes of the Tokugawa government. This brought together, shoulder to shoulder, proud men from all corners of the land, and thus fired fierce jealousies and competition. In their official duties at the shogun's court and castle, both daimyo and their retainers vied to present a superior facade, and by around 1640 virtually all had fixed upon an official family crest which they could display with optimum pride.

On a less stuffy level, the alternate-residence system permitted heraldic practice a ceremonial grandeur unprecedented during the formative years of feudal development, for it peopled the highways of Japan with ostentatious and nearly constant daimyo processionals. Engelbert Kaempfer, the Dutch scientist and trader who journeyed to the capital in 1691 and 1692, records that the entourages of the greatest lords sometimes took up to three days to pass a given point and numbered up to twenty thousand men. From Kaempfer's account, as well as from the prints and chronicles of the time, one gains a vivid impression of the carnival atmosphere of these retinues, and it is interesting to note that conspicuous among the marks of identification which they displayed were the *sashimono, umajirushi*, and *yarijirushi*, which had originally emerged as heraldic devices on the battlefield during the period of high feudalism (see page 11). The lord's crest was displayed in various places among his trappings, and his attendants wore short coats marked with a common emblem or pattern.

To ensure that retinues approaching from the opposite direction were accorded due deference (or disdain), each lord was sure to have several men among his retainers who were specially versed in such matters as crests and the various other marks of identification. Within the Tokugawa bureaucracy itself there also emerged a class of minor officials known as *gezami*, who were posted at check points along the routes to Edo and before the gates of Edo Castle and whose task, of a similar nature, was to recognize important personages immediately and command all bystanders to kneel. Those who performed these functions are the closest Japanese equivalent to the early European heralds of around the time of the tournaments in the thirteenth century. Their duties, however, remained within the realm of simple cognizance and did not develop to include any sort of professional responsibility for the recording and regulation of family emblems.

A variety of different types of books of heraldry did in fact make an appearance at this time, but all were privately and unofficially published. The most important of these were called *bukan,* literally "mirror of the warrior class," and constituted a sort of *Who's Who* of the military peerage. In addition to depicting the crests of the higher-ranking members of the warrior caste, they also included personal information about each individual, and their audience appears to have included not only the warriors themselves but also shopkeepers, creditors, and the purely curious. Crests were generally depicted in line drawings on a white background, but the *bukan* did not include any sort of description of the crests themselves comparable to the technical jargon of European blazonry. At approximately the same time as the *bukan,* other catalogues of crests began to be issued primarily for the use of artisans such as dyers and weavers who catered to the lucrative kimono trade. Generally known by the simple generic name of *moncho* (crest catalogues), these continued to be published through the Meiji era (1868–1912) and are still occasionally reproduced today. Larger in format and bolder in style than the *bukan,* crests in the *moncho* eventually came to be rendered in the *shironuki* style, that is, in white relief against a black background. These represent the true flower of Japanese heraldic design as an artistic form, and the reproductions in the present work were originally drawn several decades ago for inclusion in a never-published book of this nature.

Among the less regimented official duties performed by the warriors while in Edo was one which deserves particular mention as probably the final bastion of heraldry in all its frenetic pre-Tokugawa vigor. Each daimyo was required to assign a number of his retainers to serve as members of one of the numerous fire-fighting companies organized throughout the capital, and among these groups of deadly earnest purpose there soon emerged a temper and ritual which made this activity, in effect, a surrogate for the attractive passions and bluster of the now silenced, now nostalgic wars. Conflagrations so frequent that they soon became known by euphemism as "the flowers of Edo" plagued the new capital almost from its very inception, and a similar peril threatened all of the congested tinderbox cities and villages of the land. To a professional fighting class frustrated by days of enforced idleness and peace, fire replaced human foe as the enemy, and fire fighting became the best available warfare of the time. The fire-fighting units, composed of both warriors and commoners, were rigidly organized and drilled, and their colorful trappings included almost all of the heraldic paraphernalia which had been carried about on the battlefields of the sixteenth century. Bizarre and elaborate firemen's standards (*matoi*) identical in nature to the *sashimono* and *umajirushi* were borne by men on horseback and used to identify each individual group; small flags and lanterns marked with distinctive crests were waved in the air by men rushing to fires; helmets resembling those of warriors were worn, with large protective hoods marked with crests; and members of each unit wore distinctive, boldly patterned coats also emblazoned, in large size on the back, with crests. For most of the Edo period the flowers of Edo bloomed in profusion to provide the warrior class its sole remaining battlefield, and amidst these fumes of destruction heraldic identification in its more archaic form and setting was best preserved.

But if the system of alternate residence initially preserved and formalized heraldic practice on the one hand, on the other hand it provided the setting in which such formality could not long survive. Heraldry, observed a writer of the 1730s, "was formerly much more in Esteem than at present, as Honour itself was, which is since much sunk, and little regarded, since no Respect is given to anything but Wealth, without considering by what means it is acquired." The writer was an Englishman, James Coats, and had his survey extended to Japan he would have been able to stamp his gloom with an Oriental seal. For by the time of the happy society of the Genroku era (1688–1703), Japan—whatever its official trappings of status might be—was a land where Wealth was the equalizer and Honor of secondary concern to men intoxicated by Extravagant Pleasures. These pleasures, moreover, were dominated by two unique worlds which James Coats would have found exotic in the extreme—the Kabuki theater and the licensed quarters of the courtesans—and it was the arts and wiles of both of these places which altered the use of crests in Japan profoundly and in a manner which could not have been duplicated in Europe. In the Edo period, says a popular story of the times, a certain woman was pinched by a man and immediately produced a bruise in the shape of the plum-blossom crest of Utazaemon, a matinee idol of that day. One is hard put to find a similar tale concerning coats-of-arms in the annals of the College of Heralds.

The irreverent popular culture of late feudal Japan was known as the "floating world" (*ukiyo*), and not only did it usurp center stage from the upper classes, but it both mimicked them and was mimicked by them in turn. The Edo period was, in a sense, a society of parody, and this feature is nicely apparent in the ultimate uses and abuses to which heraldry was put. Already by 1688, the novelist Ihara Saikaku records, "Black clothing with five crests cannot be called inappropriate to anyone from daimyo down to commoners,"[1] and in an account of the rise in the world of farmers' sons he reveals pungently the extent to which this hitherto aristocratic privilege had degenerated.

> The eldest son is kept at home, but the younger ones are sent out to serve as apprentices. At first, with noses unwiped and country smells still clinging to their hands and feet, they are employed to run small errands for bean-curd or lemon flavoring. In a few years, after they have been presented with two or three sets of clothes, they are allowed to select a crest for themselves, and they start to worry about the way their hair is cut.[2]

Artisans and laborers adopted, and continue to wear, a dark blue, half-length, cotton coat known as the *shirushi banten,* on the back of which was dyed a large and often colorful crest; frequently the worker received this coat from the merchant or upper-class family who employed him, and the crest was their family mark. By the end of the Edo period, even members of the segregated *eta* class of outcasts were wearing crests.

When the townsman chose a crest for himself, he most often modeled it not after the emblem of some great warrior hero of the past but rather after the crest of a contemporary Kabuki idol, and indeed many idle warriors and their families would be scarcely half a step behind him in this emulation. With peace and leisure, and with wealth or more often just credit to go on, Edo society by the Genroku era had become consumed by a passion for fashionable and conspicuous display which suggested most strongly the elegant obsessions of the Heian court some seven hundred years before. Here, however, it was the demimonde which set the fashion. The costumes of both actors and courtesans were sumptuous, the crests they assumed were often elaborate, introducing new categories of design, and few of whatever class escaped this modish influence. "Now," wrote Ejima Kiseki, "mother and daughter alike behave immodestly: they ape the manner of harlots and courtesans, and of the actors who play female roles";[3] and it was already said of the sons and grandsons of the military heroes of Toyotomi Hideyoshi's and Tokugawa Ieyasu's campaigns that they had become more familiar with the names of the actors and prostitutes than they were with the names of the daimyo.

Thus members of many a good and high-placed family came to neglect their established family crest and wear more often than not an alternate crest modeled after that of some famous figure of the theater or licensed quarters. Sometimes the terminology with which families had previously identified their *jomon* was changed to a more elegant phrase, and some persons went so far as to alter their official family crest itself

1. Donald H. Shively, "Sumptuary Regulation and Status in Early Tokugawa Japan," *Harvard Journal of Asiatic Studies* 15 (1964–65), p. 125.

2. G. W. Sargent, trans., *The Japanese Family Storehouse* (Cambridge, 1959), p. 23.

3. Howard Hibbett, *The Floating World in Japanese Fiction* (London and Toronto, 1959), p. 100.

to make it more up-to-date. In a mockery of the conferral of crests among the upper classes, it even became common for men to bestow their own crest upon their favorite courtesan or give her gifts of clothing or bedding on which this crest was embroidered—all of which prompted a satiric haiku from the brush of the poet Kiitsu (ca. 1694–1761): "The utter collapse / Of family and fortune / Begins with crests." The "two evil places" of the theater and licensed quarters, as the novelists Ihara Saikaku and Ejima Kiseki made amply clear, were a sure, swift road to bankruptcy; and those who were frivolous with their traditional family crests, Kiitsu was saying, were those who would go on to follow this intoxicating path to ruin.

Not only did crests become a common, even essential, part of the costumes of all classes, but they were also used to embellish a variety of other items. The munificent Toyotomi Hideyoshi had set a grandiose standard of monumental heraldry comparable to the decorative display of arms in castles and cathedrals during the palmy days of European heraldry. In wood, in gold foil, in metal, in stone, his paulownia crest was worked into almost all of the many imposing castles, mansions, and temples he had built, and this practice was continued by the daimyo and shoguns of the Edo period. Edo Castle was marked with the Tokugawa hollyhock crest, and on both the castles in their domains and their mansions in Edo, it became customary for daimyo to place their family crest on such things as roof tiles, gates, pillars, transoms, outside walls, and even the stone lanterns of their gardens; old maps of Edo commonly identify daimyo residences by their crests, and when a daimyo was reassigned to a new domain, as frequently happened in the Edo period, considerable renovation of the local castles was required.

Buddhist temples and Shinto shrines were sometimes adorned with the crests of powerful families who had constructed or repaired them, and in time merchants and wealthy farmers also came to display their family emblems architecturally—in large relief, for example, on the gables of their storehouses. Outdoor parties were partitioned off from public gaze with large curtains emblazoned with crests, and carriages and palanquins were speckled with distinctive

marks; there is a full and nice continuity here, calling to mind the ox-drawn carriages of the late Heian nobility and the encampment curtains of the early Kamakura generals, on which crests had first appeared as a mark of identification. Family crests also became an invariable marking on tombstones, a practice faithfully continued to the present time. And the custom of placing a large family emblem on the sails of ships, familiar also in Europe and already done in pre-Tokugawa days, became especially conspicuous during the Edo period, when lords from the southern islands of Kyushu and Shikoku began their periodic journeys to Edo by sailing across the Inland Sea to Osaka. Fishermen and commoners whose homes were by the sea eventually took over this practice also, and in a certain district of Owari (the Nagoya area) it even became a custom to see off newly married couples in a special boat so emblazoned with the crests of both the bride's and bridegroom's families.

Rendered in immense size on architecture and the sails of ships, crests also became the delicate adornment of articles of intimate use and might be reduced to a half inch in diameter on the cover of a tiny incense case. They were used by women on such things as fans, shell combs, bronze mirrors, and ornamental bodkins—indeed some brides marked all of the articles of their trousseau with a crest much as a monogram might be used today. They also appeared on such household items as chairs, tables, chests of drawers (as metal fittings), inkstands, chopstick boxes, bowls, and wooden pillows. Again it was Hideyoshi who had set the sumptuous model for others to follow, and many of his magnificent possessions that have survived to the present time are identifiable by this use of his paulownia crest, usually worked in gold on lacquer.

In time, however, such predictable social use of crests exceeded the bounds of restraint and entered a more ambiguous realm of taste. Crackers (sembei) and small ceremonial cakes appeared in the shape of family crests, making it possible to eat one's crest and have it too, and affluent Edo gourmands could even continue on to pick their teeth with a "crest toothpick" (monyoji). Popularization and commercialization took place in almost every conceivable way, with the result that crests began to lose their associations as a mark of family identification and become little more than decoration. Shops used them as trademarks, but also applied them to such diverse goods as crockery and cosmetics. Toys appeared marked with crests, and a children's game was devised based specifically on these emblems. There even emerged a form of gambling known as *montsuke,* using the crests of actors.

And so, after centuries of turbulent development, heraldry became systematized and imbued with formal status, only to find itself almost immediately burlesqued—a plaything of fashion, a practice aped by the commoner class. No sooner had sober books of heraldry begun to be issued regularly for the warrior class but that similar volumes began to appear portraying the crests of actors and prostitutes, often in almost identical format. Little effort was made to stop these practices among the commoners, and in fact even the larger efforts of the government to prevent the disintegration of strict class lines were doomed to failure. The feudal system survived, far beyond its allotted time, until the mid-nineteenth century in Japan; it was antiquated long before this and propped up only by the most artificial and reactionary means, and the various uses of crests during the Edo period provide a small but specific picture of the developments of the time which is truer (and certainly livelier) than the crusty myths of hierarchy perpetuated officially. Crests were intimate items which finally bridged all classes, and as such they came to serve as symbols of prevailing forms and attitudes and energies—of the formal and increasingly enervated social structure on the one hand, and of the high-spirited and vital popular culture on the other.

The floating world, however, offered more than high spirits and a thin burlesque of Tokugawa officialdom. Its reproduction of the attitudes and behavior of the upper classes ran deep, and its contributions to Japanese art and design were lasting. The crests of the two evil places warrant discussion on their own right, for in bringing the development of heraldic practice full circle, they enriched both the history and the content of Japanese design.

Hideyoshi, initiator of so many of the Tokugawa traits, established the first official prostitute district in Osaka in the late sixteenth century, and by the time of the Genroku era these cities within cities had proliferated almost beyond count. The "nightless city" of the Yoshiwara in Edo alone occupied some eighteen acres of land and was populated at this time by an estimated two thousand courtesans, in addition to the thousands of other persons—attendants, musicians, jesters, servants, procurers, madams, and tradesmen—who surrounded them. Many of the women of the licensed quarters themselves knew their lives as "the world of pain" (*kugai*). To Confucian scholars and officials the quarters were an "evil place" (*akusho*)—tolerated and sponsored because it was believed they provided an outlet for passions that might otherwise turn criminal, but supposedly beneath the dignity and discipline of the warrior class. To infatuated devotees, however, the gay quarters were *gokuraku,* the Western Paradise of Amida Buddha, and discipline was rarely a match for such divine allurement.

Whatever life in the licensed quarters actually may have been, it was in its outward forms a world of great elegance and refinement, and these forms, ostensibly the product of a popular and bohemian culture, reproduced in many specific ways the attitudes and behavior of the upper classes. A hierarchy of rank and status existed among the courtesans which, although based on individual talent and accomplishments, was every bit as strict as that of the warrior class and similarly accompanied by elaborate rituals of language, costume, decorum, and privilege. A courtesan of the highest rank would expect to receive from her subordinates the same deference a daimyo received from his vassals, and the most splendid of all occasions in the quarters took place when, on several fixed days each year, a small number of the most beautiful courtesans left their respective establishments to make a solemn promenade through the streets of the district. Like the contemporaneous processions of the daimyo, these stately affairs continued until around the end of the Edo period. In rainy weather, ranking prostitutes were carried to houses of assignation on the backs of menservants and sheltered by large, long-handled umbrellas marked with their crests, a practice modeled after that of the court women (*joro,* another term for harlot, punned a similar word written with different ideographs and meaning "lady in waiting"). At night a courtesan called to another place walked through the streets of the quarter preceded by a footman carrying a great paper lantern emblazoned with her crest, surrounded by small girls, lesser prostitutes, and male attendants and entertainers, and followed by employees from the teahouses and shops, each also carrying a lighted lantern.

It was not merely luxury and license and a disrespect for traditional prerogatives which lay behind the adoption of personal crests by the courtesans, then, but a formal structure of status as well, and a flattering emulation of the practices of their social betters. Their personal crests were probably first adopted around the middle of the seventeenth century as a specific token of status by those of highest rank—as late as 1658, a popular work took special note of the fact that "Now especially, *tayu* [courtesans of the coveted uppermost rank] are putting crests on their clothing. Hassendai wears the paulownia in a wreath of flowers. She is the number one *tayu* of the Shimabara. The bellflower crest is Fujie." Soon the practice pervaded lower ranks, and eventually it even became customary for new courtesans to make their formal debut by performing a series of social visits to the various houses and shops of their quarter wearing garments especially dyed with a newly assumed crest.

Although some courtesans, such as the daughters of impoverished *ronin,* came from families with established crests of their own, their professional crests were always new and often assigned to them by the master of their house or the senior courtesan who had responsibility for them. Many such crests, however, were received from lovers, prompting one connoisseur of the quarters to caution men against making fools of themselves by being seen with a courtesan whose crest was that of another paramour. When a courtesan finished her term of service, usually around the age of twenty-six, her crest most often disappeared from view; unlike either the heraldic conventions of the warriors or the hereditary tradition which eventually developed among the Kabuki actors, these personal emblems as well as the professional names of prostitutes were only in very rare instances passed on to successors.

Many of the crests of the courtesans were characterized as *datemon,* or "dandified crests," for they possessed a greater openness of style than the emblems of the traditional system and also

varied in size depending on their use and the fashion of the time; in 1795 a sumptuary law was issued stating that *datemon* on clothing should not exceed seven inches. Sometimes they comprised two separate and distinct design elements, such as Hassendai's paulownia enclosed by a wisteria ring, in which case they were identified as *hiyoku* crests; this term derived from an imaginary pair of birds, male and female, who were joined together by a common wing and eye, and as this image suggests they were usually made by lovers combining their respective crests. Enclosures were sometimes used but frequently omitted in the courtesan crests, and the circular border in particular was poorly esteemed—"hard and inelegant" in the words of one early critic.

Despite these differences, however, many of the crests of the courtesans bore a remarkably close resemblance to those of the upper classes. Some, of course, properly belonged to these classes, having been received as gifts from lovers, but in general there was no great departure from the traditional motifs and in more than a few cases there appears to have been calculated forgery; one courtesan of the Yoshiwara actually used the imperial chrysanthemum as her crest. Paulownia, wisteria, hollyhock, crane, mandarin orange, butterfly, plum blossom, and cherry blossom—all such are present and often rendered conservatively, and a similar sense of reserve and propriety can also be noted in the ways in which courtesans used their crests. They were worn in the conventional three places or five on ceremonial kimono, placed in large size on personal lanterns and umbrellas, marked on things sent to lovers, and frequently reproduced together with the courtesan's name on the saké cups she traditionally distributed as gifts during the New Year holidays. They were not necessarily displayed on all garments, however, but appear to have been reserved for use on occasions of special formality which, in time, became fixed as set days of the year and actually known as "crest days" (*mombi*). Originally the crest days consisted of just the five national holidays, but gradually they came to include the two-week New Year's holiday and a variety of other festivals and dates fixed as special by the quarters themselves. On these days the quarters were most festive and profits greatest. Guests were expected to pay for a full day and night no matter how long they might actually stay, and the courtesans were forbidden to absent themselves for any reason—or required to compensate their master from their own purse if they did so.

Just as the complexities of the warrior society and the curiosity about it had led to the publication of guides such as the *bukan,* there also emerged beginning in the 1650's a genre of literature known as the *yujo hyobanki,* or "courtesan critiques," which dealt in a somewhat similar way with the prominent inhabitants of the licensed quarters. Many of these gave emphasis to the courtesans' crests, revealing that even they followed the practice of adopting substitute as well as formal emblems, and in several instances the *yujo hyobanki* followed the format of the *bukan* so closely that they were suppressed by the government. Where the warriors' books of heraldry had offered such information as genealogy, heir, number of retainers, and the like, the courtesans' catalogues described rank, physical features, personality, good points and bad. Where the former had listed rice stipends, the latter listed prices. As time passed, both the illustrations and commentary in these critiques became more elaborate, and they became an important link in the development of both the woodblock print and the popular *ukiyo-zoshi* novel. They also served as the fashion magazines of their day, and it was largely through this vehicle rather than through personal contact that the fashions in crests and costume became known to the general public, female as well as male.

Parallel types of publications dealing with the theater and commonly featuring the crests of actors developed alongside of the courtesans' critiques and had a similar influence on the fashions of the day. The earliest versions of these books, the *yaro hyobanki,* or "male-actor critiques," reveal that in the formative stages of the theater the young actors performed a role virtually identical to that of the courtesans. They were simultaneously entertainers and prostitutes, catering to both men and women. Homosexuality in particular had been a common and accepted practice among both the clergy and warrior caste since early in the feudal period and was known as *shudo,* "the way of the youth," a concept less mentioned but perhaps as faithfully observed as *bushido,* "the way of the warrior." Many warriors appear to have upheld sodomy as a more manly

pursuit than heterosexual relations. Thus the actors' crests which exerted so great an influence upon all strata of the Japanese population were, during the first and most vigorous century of Tokugawa rule, in large part the crests of effeminate albeit lionized youths engaged in pederasty and prostitution. Their careers were brief in moment of glory—like the courtesans of high rank, done when they were still in their twenties—and their crests, temporary fads, died with them. By the Genroku era, however, the immature vogue of the actor-prostitute had largely given way to a more diversified and legitimate form of theater which saw the emergence of truly gifted actors, and with this the beginning of actors' dynasties, the hardening of lines of hierarchy, and a more formal and lasting display of actors' crests. The status system which had pervaded the ranks of the courtesans became even more rigidly defined among the professionals of the theater, and from the Genroku era on, the public was kept informed of the precise hierarchy of the Kabuki world through the publication of striking and precisely arranged catalogues of actors' crests known as *mombanzuke,* "graded listings of crests." Other illustrated publications dealing with the theater also gave prominence to these emblems.

Many of the early Kabuki actors were *ronin,* and thus had established family crests of their own, but, like the courtesans of comparable circumstance, they did not maintain these professionally, employing instead new crests more appropriate to their public image. When plots and roles became more diversified and gave rise to stiff master-disciple relations and lines of succession, such crests assumed a permanent and hereditary character. During the Genroku era there were four Kabuki theaters in Edo, three in Kyoto, and four or more in Osaka. Together these probably employed around three hundred actors and slightly more than that number of musicians, and it was largely from this small nucleus that, through both adoption and straight blood lines, the ingrown and exclusive actors' dynasties were created, some of which have continued to the present day.

Crests used by these families sometimes derived directly from the early history of the theater. The famous three concentric squares of the Danjuro line, for example, represent three rice measures nested one in the other and were adopted as a family emblem by the first Danjuro after he had worn a costume embroidered with this mark in a widely acclaimed performance. Other actors similarly adopted as a permanent crest emblems which they had first worn in performing a specific role on the stage. The majority of these *jomon* of the Kabuki families eventually settled into a fixed collection of crests every bit as symmetrical and restrained as those of the warriors and court aristocrats, as indeed these families themselves were no less proud and haughty than their supposed social betters.

At the same time, however, the actors had a reputation for flamboyance to uphold and devised a variety of eccentric and extravagant crests which had a strong and lively influence on kimono fashions until well into the eighteenth century. Often these more frivolous emblems were used as *kaemon*, and the third Utazaemon distinguished himself as a fashion plate by using fourteen such substitute crests. Nor did idiosyncrasy cease entirely with the more sober later years of the Tokugawa rule. In the 1830's an actor named Nakamura Shikan, whose fame rested upon his expressive eyes, made ado of his forte offstage as well by using several different crests based on eyeballs.

Popular idolatry of the Kabuki actors was expressed in a number of different ways, such as the prints and various theatrical publications, and through crests entered an even more intimate realm when admirers took to placing the emblem of their favorite actor on personal articles such as clothing, mirrors, and combs. But the larger and more lasting influence of both actors' and prostitutes' crests lay in their contribution to the revolution of costume design. Their greater flexibility of style and size placed them aesthetically as a kind of bridge between the formal devices of the heraldic system and the free and brilliant patterns of Genroku kimono, and it becomes difficult to distinguish where the purpose of identification was lost and that of pure ornamentation begun.

In addition to the *datemon* and *hiyokumon* mentioned above, other types of crests also were popularized by the demimonde around the end of the seventeenth century, among them many which catered to the contemporary craze for guessing games—rebus designs, picture puzzles, and ideographs or motifs which alluded to old poems or famous views. Variegated coloring was introduced to Japanese crests for almost the first time in fanciful and effeminate emblems known as *kagamon*, and the costly tie-dyeing process which gave material a dappled effect was applied to produce crests known as *kanokomon*. Among kimono patterns there were some in which a crest repeated in small clusters, occasionally in gold thread, formed part of the larger overall design; others which consisted merely of a scattering of huge crests on a plain background; and still others in which a single decorative motif extending over the entire garment represented an elaboration of a once simple and functional heraldic device.

As heraldry per se, this development was degenerate. But as the evolution of both a form of art and a social practice, it was not only logical but felicitous. With the popularization of crests, heraldry came full circle, returning to the place from which it had derived almost a millennium before—the realm of pure decoration. Begun by a nobility beset by leisure, overfond of dress, and obsessed by a desire to be elegant and up-to-date, it ended in the hands of a class in many ways the counterpart to this, albeit an earthier aristocracy of wealth and talent. Court noble, warrior-aristocrat, entertainer, and townsman—the use of crests reflected directly the successive fortunes of these representative figures. And while the formal body of heraldic design possesses a restraint and classicism of considerable artistic merit, the departures from these forms brought a freedom and gaiety of pictorial conception which is of value in itself. The danger of such exuberance was gaudiness, of course, and sometimes the line was overstepped, but this was a small price to pay for such a liberation of spirit.

❖

The popularity of crests passed with the waning of the feudal society. All families came to have them, and then all cities, and now they are used by corporations. The circular crane flies JAL; wave-pattern crests ride cans of seaweed; the plum blossom blooms on plum wine. With the increasing popularity of Western clothing since the Meiji Restoration of 1868, the occasions for displaying personal crests have become few and largely ceremonial or commercial. They are still a part of the theater—of Noh and Bunraku as well as Kabuki—and of the geisha world in such places as the Gion of Kyoto. But the end was apparent during the final century of Tokugawa rule. It received, perhaps, its fitting benediction at a daimyo's hand in the middle of the nine- teenth century when a Dutch freighter sank in the harbor of Nagasaki. None could think of how to raise it until a farmer came and offered a workable suggestion, and for his services the lord of the region reputedly conferred upon him the crest of a Dutch hat and two tobacco pipes.

CHAPTER FIVE

Symbolism and Significance
in Japanese Heraldry

IF THE EMERGENCE of heraldry in feudal Japan was one of the by-products of a convergence of broad historical and economic and social developments, it was at the same time, on a different level, a product also of more personal occasions and preoccupations. Men originated this practice and gave it shape, and the variety of their motives and experiences found expression in the different designs, the varying motifs, which they adopted as crests. These can be grouped into a number of general categories, and while these became more clearly defined in the centuries following the Kamakura period, they were almost all implicit from the beginning. Together they reflect from different perspectives the environment in which the warrior in particular moved. They tell something of what individuals had in mind when they identified themselves with a specific crest, and placed together these various personal gestures convey a picture of the tensions and ethos and human quality of the times which is often obscured in the historian's more detached overview.

At the same time, the heraldic emblems of Japan frequently tap a deeper wellspring of Oriental imagery which derives not only from the indigenous Japanese veneration of nature but also from superstitions and religious concepts which have their origin in ancient China and even in the lands beyond the Middle Kingdom. Such prevalence of religious or quasi-religious emblems as part of the paraphernalia of war reveals that feudal thought and life in Japan were pervaded by a spiritual dimension greater than that generally ascribed by scholars to this period,

and that to a considerable extent the heraldic designs of Japan provide one excellent point of departure for gaining an insight into Japanese symbolism.

COMMEMORATIVE CRESTS

Of liveliest interest are those crests which commemorate a specific occasion of honor or martial valor. By their very nature these are also the crests whose genesis is most suspect, but still they reveal much. They mirror that pride in one's own and one's ancestors' accomplishments which never waned with time, and they provide a source of story which may be compared with the stated origins of many Western coats-of-arms.

One of the most famous of such attributions concerns the fan-with-rising-sun crest of the Nasu family, which derived from a celebrated incident during the closing stages of the Gempei War. In a classic episode recounted in the *Heike Monogatari* and still retold today in Japan to children and in the storytelling halls, the Taira forces had fled by ship to the Inland Sea, where the Minamoto caught up with them and confronted them from the shore near Yashima. Dusk was falling, and both sides were preparing to retire for the night when a small boat separated itself from the Taira fleet and drew within approximately ninety yards of the shoreline. In a gesture reflecting the courtly grace which survived even that bitter war, a young woman in the boat hung a red fan with a circular rising sun on it on a pole on the gunwale, obviously daring the Minamoto to strike it down. The task fell to one Yoichi Munetaka, a twenty-year-old son of the Nasu family and the most skillful archer among the Minamoto forces, and Yoichi, riding his horse into the shallows and praying fervently to the war god Hachiman and to the deities of his native place, loosed an arrow that struck the fluttering fan above the rivet and sent it spinning into the breeze. His descendants, with good reason, subsequently adopted as their family crest the drawing of a fan with a circular sun on it.

Less epic but more vigorous is the origin ascribed to the crest of the Niwa, once lords of Nihonmatsu in Mutsu, which is simply two crossed diagonal lines. This was said to have been adopted by an early ancestor who killed so many men in a single battle that, after wiping his sword on the left knee of his pantaloons after each encounter (as was customarily done), the bloodstains by the end of the day had formed two broad lines in the shape of an *X*. Similarly sanguinary origins are also attributed to the adoption of other commemorative crests. One warrior took as his family emblem the depiction of three dumplings on a stick, this being intended as a symbolic representation of the manner in which he had skewered the severed heads of his adversaries after killing them in battle. The decapitation of fallen foes was a common practice in feudal warfare as a means of making certain the identity of one's slain opponent, and medieval chronicles record another instance of a warrior who used the silhouette of a melon as a crest because this shape resembled the form of the pool of blood spilled after he had performed this custom on the body of a particularly renowned foe. Another and possibly less reliable commemorative attribution concerns a family which used a religious plaque as their crest motif, allegedly because one of their members had placed the heads of sixteen adversaries on such items when presenting them for identification.

The Narita family, adherents to the above-mentioned house of Niwa, used as their family crest a circle with two parallel lines drawn beside it—reputedly adopted by the founder of the family to commemorate an occasion when, having run out of provisions and faced with an imminent battle, he entered a mountain shrine, ate the offering of rice placed there, and, thus fortified, acquitted himself in the day's business with great distinction. The crest represented a rice bowl with two chopsticks laid beside it. The Nawa of Kyushu reportedly used a sailing ship as their emblem to commemorate their role in enabling the emperor Godaigo to escape his pursuers by fleeing the island by sea. And the design of two cranes facing each other which was used by the Nambu derived from an incident on the eve of this family's great victory over the Akita, when two of these auspicious birds suddenly dropped from the sky and alighted in the Nambu encampment. On a less martial line, one family used mandarin ducks as a crest motif to celebrate a skillful hunting exploit by one of their members, while another used antlers to express their pride in the physical strength of one of their men, who had torn the antlers from the head of a deer with his bare hands.

One of the most renowned and most clearly apocryphal of the commemorative crests was the three-triangle emblem displayed by the Hojo family, which occupied the apex of the feudal pyramid for over a century following the death of Minamoto Yoritomo. In the vocabulary of Japanese heraldry the triangle is conventionally identified as *uroko*, meaning fish (or dragon) scale, and the Hojo crest was said to commemorate a miraculous occurrence experienced by Tokimasa, the progenitor of the line. As the *Taiheiki* tells the story, Tokimasa had secluded himself by the sea to pray for the prosperity of his descendants, and there, in the midst of his devotions, a woman appeared before him in a dream one night to prophesy that his family would rule the land. Then she became a great serpent and disappeared into the sea, leaving behind her on the shore three large scales which Tokimasa found upon waking and adopted as a symbol on his banner.

As described elsewhere (Chapter 3), many families bore crests which had been bestowed upon them by persons of higher status—their emperor or shogun or lord—as token of a signal act of loyalty. In most cases the honored person received the right to display the crest of his benefactor, but there were also instances in which a lord personally selected a heraldic motif for one of his followers in order to commemorate a specific incident. An oblique example of this is related in the *Taiheiki* and concerns a resident of Musashi Province who was the first to join Yoritomo when the latter began his scramble for power. Promising he would be the first rewarded if the campaign was successful, Yoritomo wrote out the word "first" (*ichiban*) and gave it to the man, whose family later displayed this as their crest. The pigeon-and-mistletoe crest of the Kumagaya is also said to have been conferred by Yoritomo in commemoration of an incident in the more awkward early stages of his military career when, at the battle of Ishibashiyama (1180), he was routed and forced to flee with only a few retainers, among them Kumagaya Naozane. Hotly pursued by the Taira forces, Yoritomo hid himself in a hollow tree which was soon approached by enemy scouts. As the *Gempei Seisuiki* tells it, one of them thrust his bow into the cavity of the tree and actually touched Yoritomo's sleeve, the fugitive all the while praying to the war god Hachiman. At that very moment, two pigeons (Hachiman's symbol) burst out of the hollow tree flapping their wings loudly and causing the searchers to turn their attention elsewhere. The family records of the Kumagaya state that Yoritomo later presented them with a curtain marked with the pigeon-and-mistletoe emblem as a reward for Naozane's services "when he concealed Yoritomo in a fallen tree."

There were other types of commemorative crests as well. Among the descendants of the court nobility, one of the most famous of these was the plum blossom of the Sugawara, adopted because it was well known that this flower had been a favorite of their illustrious ancestor Michizane, a venerated figure who carved out a remarkable career at the end of the ninth century and continued to bear a heavy load of responsibility in the afterworld as Tenjin-sama, patron god of learning, poetry, calligraphy, and victims of injustice. Pride in place, the warrior's close attachment to his native soil, was also commemorated in crests, as in the flying butterfly (*fusencho*) of the Okochi, who came originally from Fusencho in Mikawa, and the oak leaf (*kaji-ba*) of the Matsura of Kaji-tani (Oak Valley) in Hirado. Another family used the *yamabuki,* or "yellow rose," because this flower grew in profusion on the riverbanks of the native village of a famous ancestor.

Martial Motifs

Although most warriors were not favored with

the talent or opportunity or the fortuitous graphic incident which would enable them to bear a specifically commemorative crest, many of them did adopt a more general kind of martial motif as both symbol of and bolster to their bellicose spirit. At first glance these crests of martial significance appear to be fewer than might be expected. The *Monten,* a recent and fairly comprehensive compilation, for example, contains approximately forty-six hundred crests, of which scarcely three percent depict articles directly related to the profession of war—arrows, arrow notches, arrowheads, bows, archery targets, battle-axes, horses and bits, flags, helmets, ornamental horns (*kuwagata*) used on helmets, and swords and sword blades.

Less immediately obvious emblems, however, also possessed martial significance. The round fan (*gumbai uchiwa*) was used by battlefield commanders to direct the movements of their troops, much in the manner in which Western officers once used a sword or baton. A thick circular pattern identified most commonly now as "snake's eye" (*janome*) was originally taken by the warrior class to be a depiction of the spool on which archers wound their bowstrings after unstringing the bow—an identification revealed in the original name of this crest, *tsurumaki-mon.* Antlers were assigned martial connotation by some because these were occasionally used to embellish the warrior's helmet. The conch shell was sometimes used as a battle trumpet, and a few individuals who took it as a crest did so with this consideration in mind. And the familiar *tomoe,* or large comma pattern, originally may have been associated with a leather band of similar shape and similar name (*tomo*) which archers wound around their left wrist to receive the shock of the released bowstring; in addition, the *tomoe* was generally used as an emblem of the war god Hachiman.

Hachiman's messenger was the pigeon, and thus even this docile bird had martial connotations when adopted as a crest by the warrior class. In a similar manner, plain circles representing stars were associated with a lesser war deity, the bodhisattva Myoken. Other predominantly religious insignia such as the Buddhist sacred wheel (*rimbo*) and a Buddhist utensil called *katsuma* were originally used as weapons in ancient India, and appear to have retained some of this original implication when adopted as heraldic designs.

On a more allegorical level, the crescent moon was likened to a bow; anchors symbolized steadfastness and staying power; the farmer's sickle was adopted by warriors for its implications of cutting down one's enemy; the mallet, traditionally associated with the god of good fortune, also suggested pulverizing one's foe; the falcon and falcon's feather brought to mind not only the popular feudal pastime of falconry, but also the image of fierce and swift attack; and the crab was selected for its "armor" and its posture of seemingly ever-ready defense. Mountains were taken as an apt symbol by men of the period of feudal wars, for on the one hand they were unyielding, and on the other they rose above their surroundings. The sea too, depicted in patterns of cresting waves, came to be assigned a special significance by brusque soldiers bound to the land. Yamanouchi Kazutoyo, lord of Tosa in the seventeenth century, is reputed to have berated one of his retainers for using a crest based on this motif on the grounds that it was effeminate and unbefitting a warrior, only to be told in reply that the movement of the waves, in their constant ebb and flow, embodied the essence of great strategy. (The retainer's own strategy here proved of mixed blessings, for his answer not only appeased his lord, but so impressed him that Kazutoyo immediately appropriated the crest for himself.)

The spirit and implements of war were also expressed in crests in other, more subtle ways, particularly by adding a stylized sword blade to the floral patterns which had been made popular by the court aristocracy. This simple and widely used device is perhaps the most resonant of all the motifs of Japanese heraldry, for in the Japanese tradition the sword was more than just a tool of the warrior's trade. Integral to the earliest mythology of the land, it was also one of the three imperial regalia. Swordmaking early became an act of devotion in Japan, and the best blades were forged by swordsmith-ascetics who underwent ritual purification before setting to their task and wore white monastic robes as they worked. The sword was thus a symbol of great violence and delicacy, particularly appropriate to the medieval period in Japan—for, like the Middle Ages of Europe, this was a time of extremes, of incredible mayhem and exquisite refinement. Apparently out of artistic considerations, Japanese draftsmen depicted in their designs not the slender, curved blade actually used on the battlefield but rather a broad, double-edged sword of Chinese origin used primarily for ceremonial functions in Japan. The sense remained the same, however, and it is this tension and counterpoint which must be read into the wood sorrel, plum blossom, and bellflower which brandish swords among their petals. In a similar manner, crests such as the calamus, Buddhist sacred wheel, and ideograph for "mountain" were sometimes imbued with obvious martial qualities by styling them in accordance with the sword-blade convention.

Other motifs of a gentle sort were also given martial significance by a subtle rendering. The docile dragonfly was one of these; commonly called *tombo,* the warriors knew it by a more archaic rendering of its name as *katsu mushi* or *shogun mushi,* "insect of victory." By an analogous pun, the water plantain (*omodaka*) became *kachi ikusa so* or *shogun so,* "plant of victory in battle."

SUPERSTITIOUS AND AUSPICIOUS CRESTS

Commemorative crests and crests of martial significance were expressions of pride, and more; they carried with them, in their adoption and perpetuation, overtones of superstition. A crest based upon a martial motif identified its bearer; it also made him more virile, reinforced the surety with which he followed his profession. The commemorative crests, including those received by conferment, became in one sense an even more tenuous sort of talisman, for the very specific nature of their origins marked them as the symbol of a peak of accomplishment. Emblems of the deeds of mighty men, they were passed on by descendants of lesser quality with a hope that fortune would continue to smile or opportunity repeat itself. Sometimes this happened, most often it did not, and crests of this nature became an increasingly reassuring tie to days of past glory.

This element of superstition was expressed directly in a number of crests which incorporated in their designs the characters for such words as great (*dai*), above (*ue*), good luck (*kichi*), profit (*ri*), fortune (*fuku*), longevity (*ju*), and myriad (*man*). An even larger category of crests was based upon auspicious motifs such as the dragonfly and plantain mentioned above or, of great popularity, the traditional symbols for longevity. Thus the crane betokened a thousand years of life; the pine, ever green, a thousand years too; and the tortoise ten thousand years of earthly residence. The plum blossom was a traditional symbol of fortitude in all the Orient, for it braves the lingering chill of winter to bloom before all other flowers. Together with the pine and bamboo, the plum blossom is known as one of the "three companions of the deep cold" (*saikan sanyu*). The bamboo, symbol of resiliency, was also associated with longevity by Chinese legend, which held that the phoenix, bird of immortality, nested in the branches of the paulownia and dined on bamboo. The paulownia, best known as one of the imperial crests but widely used among the warrior class as well, derived its significance from this same legend, while the chrysanthemum carried a similar connotation based upon Chinese tales of a class of mountain hermits who survived to hoary age by subsisting solely upon a diet of this flower. The handsome chrysanthemum-on-water crest of Kusunoki Masashige, Godaigo's masterful general, was based directly upon a variation of this legend which told of a village in the mountains of China so overgrown with chrysanthemums that the blossoms floated on the mountain stream and the villagers, because they drank of these waters, rarely died before they reached a hundred. As such examples indicate, the Chinese tradition contributed greatly, not only to the patterns of Japanese heraldry, but also to the interior sense of many of these patterns.

Other motifs familiar to Japanese heraldic design carried less obvious or less well-known auspicious connotations, some of which derived from ancient folk practices. Both the fern (*shida*) and shrimp, for example, were displayed during New Year's ceremonies—the former because, like the pine, it remains green even in deep snow; the latter, according to some accounts, because it resembles an old man, bent over and bearded, and thus betokens longevity. Cloves were good luck symbols, possibly because of their early use for medicinal purposes, and similar associations applied to shepherd's purse. Hemp leaves and bundles of cotton were used in early times as re-

ligious offerings, while holly and a bow made from the wood of the peach tree were used in rites of exorcism; the iris was also used in Heian times as protection against evil spirits. The giant radish (*daikon*), particularly a forked radish, was ascribed powers relating to fertility. The mallet was traditionally associated with Daikoku, one of the Seven Gods of Good Fortune, and it was believed that a shake of the mallet caused one's wishes to be fulfilled. The curious round shape known as *suhama* derives from the shape of a popular tray landscape first used at banquets in the Heian period. Associated with a mythological island named Horaijima, where people never died, the tray was decorated with most of the traditional symbols of longevity (crane, tortoise, pine, bamboo, plum, and the like) and sometimes included the figures of an old man and woman. As a heraldic motif, the *suhama* shape carried this same auspicious connotation and enjoyed extremely great popularity. By a rather charming conceit, even the folding fan was made an emblem of good luck, symbolizing "expanding prospects."

Several items assumed auspicious connotations rather late in the feudal period. The wood sorrel, for example, was belatedly ascribed propitious qualities based on the fact that it produces numerous seeds and reproduces itself easily; thus it became a token of future progeny and prosperity. Ivy found favor as a motif among courtesans because of its resemblance to the symbiotic nature of their own lives: both cling to others to survive. And coins were apt to be adopted as crests because of the ideographs they bore depicting the period in which they were first minted; such period names (*nengo*) invariably were made up of auspicious characters.

A number of crests derived auspicious qualities from more or less far-fetched puns. Some of these involved plays on sound or pronunciation, others involved alternative readings for the ideographs used or alternative terms of identification along the lines of the previously mentioned dragonfly and water plantain. Thus the rice measure, *masu*, could be written with a different ideograph meaning "increase," and by a comparable substitution of ideographs zingiber (*myoga*) became "divine protection"; a fern known as *nagi* became "to pacify"; the decoration used on gifts (*noshi*) became "to spread out"; the circular pattern known as *shippo,* literally "four directions," became "seven treasures"; and sedge headgear (*kasa*) became "increase" or "enlarge." The homely trivet (*gotoku*), by virtue of the very ideographs with which it was written, already meant the five Confucian virtues. By an alternate reading, the battle-axe (*ono*) became *yoki* or "good." By fracturing the language somewhat more severely, the radish (*daikon*) was given a Sinified reading of *raifuku* which subsequently could be given new ideographs meaning "come fortune," while the gingko (*icho*) became "barbarians pay tribute." A popular diamond-shaped motif identified for already complicated etymological reasons as *kuginuki* or "nail extractor" underwent a powerful metamorphosis to emerge as "pulling up nine castles." The most outlandish of all heraldic puns, however, involved the bird-shaped comb known as *akadori* or "red bird," a play on a very different *akadori* meaning "dandruff remover"—a desirable objective, perhaps, but more reflective of personal idiosyncrasy than of Japanese culture.

Religious Crests

The same attitude which encouraged the adoption of superstitious and auspicious crests turned also in a more specifically religious or quasi-religious direction and found expression in the use of emblems derived from Shinto, Buddhism, Christianity, Confucianism, and rites of incantation. Of these beliefs, that which exerted by far the greatest influence upon the content of family crests was the indigenous cult of Shinto, the "Way of the Gods." Many crests depicted objects which were sacred to Shinto ritual or unique to the architecture and environment of the shrine, such as bells, urns, mirrors, plaques, amulets, paper pendants, picket fences, the ornamental cross beams and ridgepole of the shrine gable, and the familiar *torii,* or shrine gateway. Both the oak and the cryptomeria, and to a lesser extent the gingko, were held in special veneration by Shinto—largely because these trees are commonly found growing in shrine compounds—and this encouraged the design of a number of crests based upon the leaves of these trees. The influence of the native cult also appeared, less obviously but perhaps even more pervasively, in the representation of flora and fauna which were associated with specific deities or shrines, as well as in the adoption by the faithful of crests based upon the emblem of the shrine to which they paid allegiance—for once the custom of using crests as a mark of identification had begun, it found most avid practitioners among the local Shinto establishment.

The predominant influence of Shinto among the religious motifs of Japanese heraldry is particularly interesting given the fact that Shinto was weak in institutional organization, negligible in iconography, and perhaps unparalleled in doctrinal obfuscation. Nevertheless, the warrior class evinced through its heraldic emblems strong attachment to native shrines and particular attachment to those numerous establishments dedicated to the worship of Hachiman, the god of war. Below Hachiman, the deities of the Kumano, Suwa, and Mishima shrines, and Tenjin of the Temman Shrine, were held in particular veneration by men engaged in war.

Several families used pigeons in their family crest, since these were Hachiman's messengers; the association was not all that illogical when one considers that pigeons were undoubtedly the bird most often seen on shrine premises. Other families used the *tomoe,* with which Hachiman was also associated. To a lesser extent, some parishioners based their crests on the "messengers" of their local shrines, such as the deer of Kasuga, monkey of Hiyoshi, raven of Kumano, and tortoise of Matsuo and Izumo. Among the plants and trees represented in crests specifically because of their associations with particular shrines were the cryptomeria of Miwa; hollyhock of Kamo and Tosho; oak of Kumano, Kasuga, and Izu; and paper mulberry of Sumo. Worship of Tenjin (the deified Sugawara Michizane) was widespread throughout the land, and many who adopted the plum blossom as a family crest did so because of its association with this patron deity.

Other motifs also entered the realm of personal heraldic identification because of their particularistic associations with Shinto. These included the sickle crest of Suwa; falcon's feathers of Higo and Aso; hexagon (carapace) and ideograph 有 ("existence") of Izumo; amulet of Kyoto's Yasaka (Gion) Shrine; and ideograph for "three" in an enclosure of Oyamazumi. As the above notations reveal, single shrines often had numerous specific associations which their parishioners might adopt as a personal crest; the Kumano Shrine, for example, was associated with crests depicting the raven, rice plant, *nagi* fern, wisteria, paper pendant, and Shinto bells. Some families also indicated their faith by using as their crest one of the ideographs which appeared in the name of a god or shrine, such as *hachi* 八, the first character of Hachiman 八幡. The prevalence of this practice of basing family crests upon the emblems or symbols of a local shrine or deity was great enough to result in a marked geographic concentration of certain motifs in certain areas.

Crests of Buddhist significance were far fewer than those based on Shinto motifs, and this is not necessarily what might have been anticipated, for although Shinto was the native cult and officially the state religion, Buddhism was more splendid and sophisticated and tightly organized, and was, in all but name, the true religion of the land. In the final analysis, however, the predominance of Shinto over Buddhist influence in the selection of crests among the warriors most probably derived, not so much from any institutional strength, but rather from the more muted and deeper strains of the Japanese spirit to which traditional Shinto, more than Buddhism, was attuned. The this-worldly aspect of Shinto and the closeness of its tie to nature struck a chord of great response among men whose concerns were of this world and whose roots were in the land. The entire body of Japanese family crests is distinguished by simplicity and directness; it is dominated overwhelmingly by designs drawn from nature, and particularly plants and trees, and this sort of concreteness was Shinto's province. Buddhism, other-worldly, abstract, and ornate, answered to another kind of need. It was not sufficient in itself, and clearly did not provide the kind of symbolism which could be adopted quite so handily by men whose profession was war.

The most conspicuous of the Buddhist motifs used on crests was the *rimbo,* or sacred wheel, which had been introduced to Japan in the early ninth century with the esoteric practices of the Shingon and Tendai sects. This was a symbol which operated on many levels, its sense residing in the image of the wheel turning freely and crushing all obstacles; it represented the teachings of the Buddha, for example, which broke down the obstacles in one's mind, and was used in the initiation ceremonies of priests. The warriors appear to have worn it as a crest, however, largely with the more mundane intention of soliciting divine assistance as they rolled over terrestrial foes. Several of the utensils used in Buddhist ceremony also provided a motif for crests, especially the *katsuma,* used to exorcise devils, and the *shakujo,* believed to provide protection against wild beasts and poisonous snakes. The Buddhist swastika, emblem of great luck and boundless virtue, appeared in various forms on a number of warrior crests. Patterns made up of circles representing stars also were sometimes used because of their associations with the bodhisattva Myoken, a god of war with particular associations with the Ursa Major (Big Dipper) constellation. Such usages as these were more superstitious than religious in their import, and there are only a few crests which actually touched upon the profounder aspects of the faith; one of these was based upon the ideograph *mu* 無 (nothingness, or void) and reflected the teachings of the Zen sect.

More tenuous Buddhist associations also appear among the heraldic designs of Japan. These include the gong and the dragon, both associated particularly with Zen; the centipede, associated with the north and assigned the role of retainer to one of the four Buddhist guardians of the four directions; the radish, often associated with the elephant-headed god Shoten in Buddhist iconography; the conch shell and large axe, both of which are used for both practical and esoteric purposes in mountain asceticism; the lotus, a pivotal Buddhist symbol representing the emergence of purity out of impurity; and the peony, which had particular associations with certain temples such as the Kofuku-ji, Daijo-in, Hongan-ji, and Soji-in. In the latter part of the feudal period, it became customary to place six coins by the body of a dead person to enable him to pay the tolls on his passage to the afterworld, and a number of families sought to assure themselves safe passage by using a depiction of six coins as their family crest.

The influence of Christianity and Confucianism upon heraldic design was late in appearing and never approached that of Shinto or even

Buddhism in extent. The Christian cross began to appear as a crest after Francis Xavier's mission to Japan in 1549, and was particularly conspicuous around the Settsu area of Kyushu, where converts were most numerous. Most of the different Western versions of the cross were known and used in this way, and these together with Christian inscriptions were prominently displayed in several of the greatest military episodes of the sixteenth and early seventeenth centuries. The renowned convert Konishi Yukinaga led a predominantly Christian army beneath banners marked with the cross during the ill-considered Japanese invasions of Korea in 1592 and 1597, for example, and a number of the warriors who unsuccessfully defended Osaka Castle against Tokugawa Ieyasu in 1615 were converts who inscribed Christian insignia on their flags. As described by C. R. Boxer, Padre João Rodriguez Girão recorded that at this latter battle "There were so many crosses, Jesus and Santiagos on the flags, tents, and other martial insignia which the Japanese use in their encampments, that this must needs have made Ieyasu sick to his stomach." Even this, however, was not the high point of the display of Christian emblems in Japan. In the celebrated Christian-led uprising at Shimabara from 1637 to 1638, some thirty thousand men, women, and children fought beneath almost exclusively Christian banners, some inscribed in Portuguese, until they were massacred with but a single reputed survivor.

At its peak, around 1615, the Christian movement may have numbered as many as five-hundred thousand converts, but the persecutions which began in the early seventeenth century and culminated at Shimabara shattered this momentum and forced the movement underground, making any further open display of the cross impossible. Some of the "hidden Christians," however, nevertheless continued to affirm their faith by assuming family emblems in which the cross was disguised in a design of greater complexity. The already established crest known as the *Gion mamori,* which depicted the amulet of the Yasaka (Gion) Shrine, was widely used in this way by converts such as the devout Ikeda families of both Bizen and Inaba, for it contained within its design a happenstance but quite exact rendering of the St. Andrew's cross. Other hidden crosses were displayed in the form of crossed oars or

arrow notches, or as horses' bits and possibly even as the Buddhist swastika.

Confucianism, although established as a major area of classical studies in Japan as early as the Nara period, does not appear to have had any direct influence upon the content of Japanese crests until the time of the neo-Confucian revival of the Edo period, a time when in general the system of heraldry in Japan was settling down into a pattern built upon some four centuries of customary practice. At that late date the number of Confucian motifs adopted was small, and, interestingly, drawn almost exclusively from the more occult aspects of this philosophy—the triangles and hexagrams of the *I Ching,* for example, and the circular light-and-dark symbol of the Absolute (*taikyoku*). The very esoteric nature of these emblems in itself, however, suggests that it may be somewhat misleading to see so clean a chronological break as regards the Confucian influence, for there was no clear dichotomy between Confucianism and the Chinese practices of geomancy, divination, and incantation which had, from an earlier date, contributed some signs and tokens to the general body of heraldic design in Japan.

These signs sound depths of mysticism, but it is probably not unjust to say that these ultimate meanings also were not grasped in detail even by those who turned in this direction in selecting a motif for their crest. Here again the atmosphere of crisis which hung over the warrior's existence, and the attempt to counter this by charms and propitious marks, was undoubtedly the major consideration behind the selection of emblems of an occult or mystical nature. The most common of these signs was simply two lines drawn in the shape of a cross (*jumonji*), a primitive mark of sorcery found in almost every country and used to exorcise demons and summon fortune. The character for the number nine was adopted as a crest by several families because this was the number assigned to *yang,* the dynamic, masculine force of the cosmic *yin-yang* dualism; although the character for the number eight was used on certain crests either because of its associations with Hachiman or because it appeared in the family name of the user of the crest, the fact that this was also the number assigned to the passive and feminine force of *yin* does not appear to have been regarded as significant. The traditional *yin-*

yang symbol itself was known in Japan and reproduced there, but does not appear to have been used as a formal family crest. Another emblem, the *kagome,* which derives its name from the mesh of a woven basket and duplicates the Star of David, was used because of its powers of exorcism—powers similarly ascribed to the *Abe Seimei han,* a pictograph identical to the pentagram with which Faust confronted Mephistopheles and which is still used in Japan today on the clothes of newborn infants; the name literally meant "the seal of Abe Seimei," and referred to Japan's most famous geomancer, who lived in the mid-Heian period. Several families used a plaque with the ideographs for "twenty-eight" written on it, a reference to the twenty-eight parts into which ancient geomancers divided the celestial sphere. Another motif along these same lines was based on rectilinear stripes identified as *sangi* and denoting in some cases a popular method of divination involving wooden sticks.

CRESTS OF DENOTATION, CRESTS OF BEAUTY

Warrior crests generally fall within the previous categories; those of the court nobility more often belong to one of two other general groupings. The first comprises what are known as denotative or indicative crests, which either present directly, or more often suggest, the surname of their bearers; the second consists of crests selected primarily because of their elegance, their beauty and effectiveness as design per se. The division by social class is a very loose and general one, however, for the warriors also proved adept at tastefulness and patronymics, while the courtiers were hardly strangers to the occult and divine.

Crests of a denotative nature assumed a variety of forms, for they derived not merely from the desire to display one's name, but also from certain qualities of the Japanese language itself— the calligraphic beauty of the individual character, the multiple meanings of single sounds, and the fact that a large percentage of Japanese family names are written with ideographs which have an independent and often pictorial meaning of their own. Many of these names are drawn, in part or whole, directly from nature; *tsuru* (crane) and *tachibana* (mandarin orange) are familiar surnames in themselves, for example, while *fuji*

(wisteria), *matsu* (pine), *yama* (mountain) and *kawa* (river) are among the most common elements used, together with another ideograph, for family names. Thus Fujiwara means literally, "field of wisteria," and Yamanouchi is "within the mountains." Other names include the ideographs for such words as *ta* (rice paddy) and *i* (well crib), and bespeak the tasks to which primitive man first turned his hand when he became a shaper himself of his environment. Of abstract ideographs used in family names, several, such as *dai* or *o* (great), *ka* (increase), *ue* (above), and *kyu* (nine, representing the cosmic force *yang*) are of auspicious meaning in themselves, and thus could serve double purpose when rendered in a family crest. As a result the denotative crests are by no means as confined or straightforward as their label might at first suggest.

Most often a surname was suggested by utilizing just one of its ideographs. This might be rendered calligraphically in any of a number of styles, including abstract versions. The ideograph might appear alone or be incorporated with a purely decorative motif; only rarely were both ideographs of a surname used together to form a crest. Where one of the elements of the name was pictorial, this was frequently drawn representationally; over thirty families whose names included *i* used variations of a well-crib design as their crest, while a similar number of families with *fuji* as a part of their names used the wisteria. In some cases the entire name was conveyed by combining calligraphy and design, as in the crest of the Kato family, where the character for *ka* was enclosed in a circular wisteria pattern (*to* is the Chinese reading for wisteria). A more subtle denotative crest along similar lines was adopted by the Goto family, whose name literally means "five wisteria"; they enclosed a single rectangular stripe in a wisteria ring, because in an ancient method of arithmetic calculation known as *sangi,* a single piece of wood placed horizontally was, by definition, equivalent to five units. The pine (*matsu*) was used by families such as the Akamatsu and Matsuo; the cryptomeria (*sugi*) by families such as the Sugi, Sugita, and Uesugi; and the bamboo (*take*) by such families as the Kotake and Takenouchi. An entirely pictorial surname such as Tsuru, Tachibana, Kaji, or Torii might be conveyed by crests depicting the crane, mandarin orange, oak leaf, or Shinto gateway respectively.

More allusive denotation was also possible. Thus the rice plant (*ine*) was adopted as a heraldic motif by numerous families whose surnames in one way or another were connected with rice cultivation; among these were the Yonekura ("rice storehouse"), Yoneno ("rice field"), Inatomi ("rice-plant abundance"), Shimmomi ("new unhulled rice"), Okada ("hill paddy"), and Ikeda ("pond paddy"). A branch of the Suzuki family in the Kii region used the rice plant for one of their crests because in the ancient dialect of their district their name sounded the same as a word meaning "pile up rice"; at the same time this family also used another crest depicting Shinto bells (*suzu*), a straightforward denotation of the first ideograph used in writing their surname. A small number of denotative crests were based on puns and homonyms. The Komakine family, for example, whose name literally meant "horse tree root," used a pestle (*kine*) for their family crest, while the Emi family use the shrimp (*ebi*) to convey a kind of contrapuntal phonetic denotation. A more literary type of allusion was utilized by the Yoshino family, who took the cherry blossom as a heraldic motif because in the fixed poetic conventions of Japan this immediately called to mind the springtime slopes of Mt. Yoshino.

The designs which had been used by the nobility on their garments and carriages and household furnishings during the Heian period appeared as the distinctive marks of these families with increasing frequency during the Kamakura period, but it was not until the seventeenth century, with the periodic publication of a genealogy of the nobility known as the *Unjo Meiran,* that these crests were gathered together. This collection reveals how great was the rule of taste and style among this class, for although a number of their crests were of a denotative nature, and some of their favorite motifs, such as the plum blossom, chrysanthemum, and crane, may have had ulterior significance, their basic and overriding criterion was clearly that of decorative beauty. Among the crests selected by both the court aristocracy and the warrior class with this consideration uppermost in mind were those based on motifs such as the butterfly, wild goose, plover, moon and snowflake, and—far and away predominant—plants and flowers such as the wisteria, cherry blossom, gentian, peony, mandarin orange, maple leaf, ivy, iris, wood sorrel, bellflower, clove, passion flower, spatterdock, bracken, mistletoe, pampas grass, and reed. Traditional Chinese patterns such as those based on the diamond or lozenge shape and the popular "China flower" (*karabana*) and "melon" (*mokko*) were also selected primarily because of their symmetry and courtly connotations. Other motifs selected primarily because they evoked an idealized image of the elegant life included the carriage wheel, folding fan, umbrella, and drum. Even the plain clam shell was considered one of the "crests of beauty," for it was associated with several genteel pastimes of the Heian court society.

HERALDIC DESIGN AND THE JAPANESE HIERARCHY OF VALUES

Almost all Japanese family crests reveal, in the considerations which underlay their selection, a personal concern or predilection or experience which permits their being spoken of in terms of one of the categories described above. There is, of course, overlap. Martial crests were almost a priori superstitious, for example, and a denotative crest might well have auspicious connotations. And because the Japanese as a race are gifted with both the awareness of and the touch of beauty, there are few crests which do not reveal, in line and grace of balance, a fine aesthetic concern. Designs, no matter what their significance might be, were generally rendered simply and with restraint, and while this was consistent in part with the considerations of military expediency which prompted the first wholesale adoption of crests, it was also consistent with one of the fundamental canons of Japanese taste. This was by no means an exclusive canon, for there is also in the Japanese temper a fancy for the lavish and ornate which was manifested in some of the patterns of the Heian period, in certain flamboyant excesses of the later warriors, and in the more dandified crests popularized by actors and prostitutes in the Edo period. In general, however, the family crests of the Japanese reveal a distaste for clutter and an awareness of the effectiveness of small things simply presented which is characteristic of all of their finest artistic expressions, whether in poetry or architecture, painting or tea.

Apart from the ulterior significances behind their selection, the very subjects which the Japanese chose to draw on their crests reveal something of their outlook as a people, for the vast majority of these come from the inanimate world of nature, and then from among small physical objects, and then geometric forms. Motifs drawn from the animate world are comparatively few. Birds and insects are favored over animals, and animals over mankind; neither man nor parts of the human anatomy appear at all in the mainstream of Japanese crests, as they sometimes do in European heraldry. Very possibly there is something larger to be read in this—a hierarchy of values almost the antithesis of that of the West, a world where the stillness of nature, the inanimate form, speaks strongest to the heart.

Part Two

Crests and Commentaries

Heaven and Earth

1-10. Cloud (*kumo*). The cloud pattern appears to have been brought to Japan in connection with Buddhist teachings, symbolizing the realm beyond or the spirits of the dead. As a crest it maintained these religious connotations, and was adopted by some Buddhist and Shinto practitioners—as indicated by the cloud and Shinto pendant design below (9). At the same time, the pattern carries the connotation of elegance and high status; from early times, for example, Japanese courtiers were poetically referred to as "Gentlemen Who Dwell Among the Clouds" (*kumo no uebito*) because of their close association with the throne. The stylized moon-and-cloud motif (8) is used as a basic enclosure for Japanese crests.

11-30. Lightning (*inazuma*). This pattern is known to have been used in China during the Chou dynasty (eleventh to fifth centuries B.C.), although it is not clear when it became identified as a depiction of lightning. Its transition to Japan and use as a crest there is not well documented, but only a small number of families had adopted it as a family emblem by the Edo period. The martial connotations of the lightning emblem are unmistakable, and in all probability the pattern carried religious connotations as well. One of the religious implements used in the Shingon sect of Buddhism, which flourished in Japan, for example, is the *vajra* or symbolic thunderbolt. The very ideographs with which *inazuma* is written suggest a quasi-religious dimension, for literally they mean "rice-plant wife," suggesting fecundity and the basic forces of life.

31-35. Mist (*kasumi*). The stylized rendering of mist is a familiar convention in Japanese scroll paintings and was belatedly adopted as a crest by certain actors' families.

36-50. Moon (*tsuki*). One of the most familiar poetic images of Japan, the moon was used as a design or crest not only for its elegant associations, but also in some cases for religious or even martial reasons. Many epithets play with this imagery. Thus elegant prose and poetry was described as *fugetsu,* "wind-moon"; Kyoto in ancient times was known as *Tsuki no miyako,* City of the Moon, in reference to the imperial presence there; and in Buddhism, the moon symbolized wisdom or the Buddhist law, and one reads of the "moon of enlightenment." On August 15, aristocrats and later commoners also celebrated "The Great Moon-Viewing," a festival which originated in China. Those versed in Chinese geomancy knew the moon as a manifestation of *yin,* the passive female force of the universe, while Buddhists associated the moon with the bodhisattva Myoken. Warriors took the crescent, or "three-day" moon, as an emblem because of its resemblance to a bow.

Many of the most familiar lunar associations are depicted in the crests below, such as the moon and stars (37–40, 46, 47), cloud (41), flowing water (42), wild goose (49), and plum blossom (50). The association of moon and rabbit (48) derives from Japanese mythology. Among the less obvious versions are "hazy moon" (43), moon and latticework (44), and moon and rice measure (45).

51-75. Mountain (*yama*). Since Japan is so mountainous that less than one-fifth of the land can be tilled, it is only natural that mountains form a familiar image of both the written and visual arts. More than that, however, mountains provided clear and apt symbolism for the ambitious and forceful warriors of the feudal period. In the passive-active dualism of the *yin-yang* cosmology, mountains were *yang* to the *yin* of the rivers. Unyielding, unmoving, they carried an unmistakable martial connotation. High, reaching to the heavens, they also augured well for men of ambition.

The crest depicting Mt. Fuji (51), for example, meant "highest in the land"; it was used by the Aoki family, with more vim than veracity. Since *yama* is an exceptionally common part of many Japanese surnames mountain crests also frequently had denotative significance.

The mountain designs provide a good example of the Japanese genius for abstraction and variation. The last five crests depict variations on the ideograph for mountain (71, enclosed in a circle), and two of these (74, 75) heighten the martial aspects by styling the center stroke of the ideograph as a sword blade.

76-95. Snow (*yuki*). Although the snowflake was not one of the dominant motifs among Japanese crests, the stylized "snow ring" enclosure (91–95) became a popular and elegant convention. Apart from its obvious beauty, snow was also regarded as an auspicious sign of a bountiful year to come—possibly because winter snows meant spring rivers and fertilization of the soil. In early Japanese court society, the year's first snowfall became the occasion both for festive snow-viewing parties and for official meetings to decide appointments for the coming year. Centuries later, in the pleasure quarters of Edo, the

first snow also was celebrated as an occasion of particular note. "Since there were years in Edo in which no snow fell," according to one source, "the first snowfall was greatly admired. Men accompanied geisha on boats to view the snowfall, and invited honored guests to tea ceremonies in the snow. The brothels used the snow as an excuse for making guests stay longer, and the saké shops took the snow as an auspicious sign of guests soon to come."

96-110. Stars (*hoshi*). Superstitious Japanese of the Nara and Heian periods took readily to the astrology and geomancy of the Chinese tradi-

tion, and stars played a conspicuous role in this tangled spiritual realm. Each person had his own particular guardian star, determined by his date of birth. Similarly, certain stars and constellations had their own particular associations and were believed capable of exerting protective influence. Picture scrolls of these early centuries reveal the circular "star" pattern to be one of the most common motifs on the costumes and carriages of the aristocracy.

The design was further popularized by the warrior class, and for similar reasons: it was auspicious, graceful, and easy to identify. A depiction of

three stars, for example, was associated with Orion and called the "three warriors" or "stars of the generals" in both Chinese and Japanese. In a similar manner, seven or more stars were associated with worship of Ursa Major, a practice adopted from China in the early Heian period and gradually worked into Buddhist belief—and particularly belief in the protective war deity Myoken.

The five-pronged star of Western pictorial convention had little place in the heraldry of the East, but see 2671.

111-15. Sun (*hi*). The circular red "rising sun" first appeared as a popular decorative pattern on fans in the early Heian period. It was not adopted as a national emblem until 1854, and the Japanese "rising sun" flag was not designed until 1870. Even as an imperial symbol, the sun was not conspicuously emphasized until around the beginning of the thirteenth century, when gold and silver embroidered circles representing the sun and moon respectively were displayed on the emperor's brocade banners. The solar symbol derived, of course, from Japan's legendary origins and the alleged genesis of the imperial line from the Sun Goddess. Despite its belated formalization as an imperial and then national emblem, however, surprisingly few families adopted the sun, or sun-and-sun-rays, as a family emblem.

116-25. Wave (*nami*). One of the more dynamic of the Japanese heraldic motifs, the wave design appears to have become particularly popular after the twelfth century. In addition to its elegance, warriors used it as a symbol of power and resilience. Yamanouchi Kazutoyo, lord of Tosa in the seventeenth century, is reputed to have berated one of his retainers for using a crest based on this motif on the grounds that it was effeminate and unbefitting a warrior, only to be told in reply that the movement of the waves, in their constant ebb and flow, embodied the essence of great strategy. (The retainer's own strategy here proved of mixed blessings, for his answer not only appeased his lord, but so impressed him that Kazutoyo immediately appropriated the crest for himself.) The last crest below (125) combines the attributes of wave, whirlpool, and the ancient and auspicious *tomoe* design (*see* 2531–65).

101 102 103 104 105
106 107 108 109 110
111 112 113 114 115
116 117 118 119 120
121 122 123 124 125

Plants, Flowers, and Trees

126-30. Arrowroot (*kuzu*). Known as one of the "seven plants of autumn," arrowroot is particularly associated with the Yoshino area near Kyoto, where special products such as medicine, starch, and cloth were made from its roots and stem.

131-90. Bamboo (*take*). Versatile, graceful, and auspicious, from ancient times bamboo has played an extraordinarily large role in Japan. Originally brought from China to grace the gardens of the Japanese nobility, approximately 150 varieties are now estimated to exist in the country. The strength and flexibility of bamboo has taken it far from the nobility's gardens over the centuries: fences, lattices, ladders, and pipes; arrows and spears; flutes and writing brushes; baskets, brooms, hats, and sieves are merely a few of its daily guises.

The bamboo has admirable connotations. Along with the pine and plum blossom, it is known as one of the "three companions of the deep cold," and its endurance throughout the seasons has caused it to be associated with such virtues as constancy, integrity, and honor. At the same time, from Chinese mythology the bamboo became closely identified with both the phoenix and the paulownia—for the regal (and finicky) phoenix was said to rest only on the branches of the paulownia and dine only on the seed of the bamboo. Based on this legend, the Chinese developed intricate patterns incorporating the phoenix, paulownia, and bamboo, and these were subsequently imported from T'ang China and displayed on the court costumes of the Japanese aristocracy. Perhaps through these associations, the bamboo is also a symbol of purity and nobility in Japan.

Beginning with this early use as an embroidered design on court costumes, the bamboo soon became

singled out as an attractive pattern in its own right. It appears in many of the picture scrolls of the Heian period, and began to be used as a carriage crest around the beginning of the Kamakura period. Among warriors of the middle ages, the bamboo proved to be one of the most popular marks of identification, and by the Edo period, it was in widespread use among the nobility as a family crest.

The majority of patterns based on bamboo depict some variation on the bamboo leaf (126–60), and this popularity reflects not only the connotations of the bamboo itself, but also the practice of subtle mimicry which was common in Japanese heraldry. In the feudal period in particular, many warrior families adopted the bamboo leaf as an emblem because of its resemblance to the gentian crest worn by the most eminent of warrior clans, the Seiwa Genji. The Kotake and Takenouchi families adopted the bamboo crest for denotative reasons. Other designs focus upon the stem of the bamboo (161–75); bamboo shoots (176–79, 188), a great culinary delicacy in Japan; and stylized versions of cut bamboo (183–84). Some of the more poetic and auspicious associations of the bamboo are depicted in the last crests in this selection: bamboo and sedge hats (179–82); a bamboo ring and paper crane (185); plum blossom and bamboo leaf (186); mock paulownia designs composed of snow and bamboo leaf (187), bamboo shoots and paulownia leaf (188), and bamboo leaf, plum blossom, and stylized pine (189); and a last design depicting the three companions of the deep cold—bamboo, plum blossom, and pine (190). (*See also* 1442–48.)

191-225. Bellflower (*kikyo*). The *kikyo* or *Platycodon grandiflorum*—translated variously as Chinese balloon flower or broad bellflower—is a five-petal, indigo flower which blooms in August and is known as one of the "seven plants of autumn." Originally a wildflower found particularly in the Yoshino area, it was gradually domesticated and brought into private gardens. As a crest, it first appears to have been adopted among the warriors around the thirteenth century, primarily because of its beauty. As the selection below reveals, the bellflower is one of the Japanese design motifs most adaptable to variation. The last four crests below illustrate the fanciful conventions often used by Japanese artists when working with floral designs: the bellflower has undergone a metamorphosis to become, in order, a crab, two butterflies, and a crane.

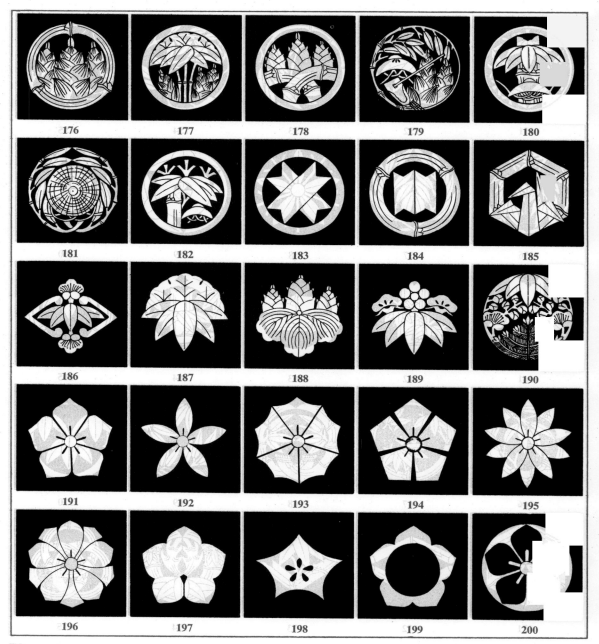

226-35. Bracken (*warabi*). The new shoot of bracken that emerges in early spring is likened by the Japanese to a fist (by the name *warabide*, bracken-hand). This became the basis of a fairly popular pattern used on household items, and a small number of families eventually adopted the motif as a family crest. The bracken designs below are a good example of the wide variations possible on a single theme.

236-37. Calamus (*shobu*). A rare motif, the calamus design conveys a martial impression both by its suggestion of a sword blade and by the fact that the Japanese word *shobu*

puns on words of identical sound meaning "martial spirit" and "victory or defeat."

238-73. Cherry Blossom (*sakura*). Japanese admiration of the cherry blossom can be traced back to the very earliest written classics, the *Kojiki* and *Nihon Shoki,* but the bloom does not appear to have established itself as a kind of "national flower" until around the tenth century. In the great eighth-century poetic anthology, the *Man'yoshu,* for example, the cherry blossom is alluded to much less frequently than the bush clover or plum blossom. By the time of the second great anthology, the tenth-

century *Kokinshu,* however, the cherry blossom had far outstripped the other blooms as a favorite theme. This new appreciation of a native product coincided with a larger cultural transition away from the standards of the Chinese tradition toward more indigenous values and images. To give one example, the special popularity of the cherry blossom developed at approximately the same time that the purely native school of painting known as *Yamato-e* merged. From the tenth century on, the cherry blossom was so obvious a favorite that in both poetry and prose it was conventionally referred

226 227 228 229 230
231 232 233 234 235
236 237 238 239 240
241 242 243 244 245
246 247 248 249 250

to simply as "the flower," or *hana*.

Originally found wild in the foothills around Nara and Kyoto, the cherry tree was soon planted in the formal gardens of Kyoto. Both single-bloom and double-bloom varieties were cultivated (for the latter, see 240 and 244 below). Beginning around the tenth century, annual blossom-viewing ceremonies were held by both the court and various religious establishments. The famous *Pillow Book* by Sei Shonagon contains a particularly famous section describing a blossom-viewing excursion taken by the ladies of the court. Paintings of the late Heian period such as the *Eiga Monogatari* picture scroll reveal the popularity of the cherry blossom as a pattern on clothing and utensils, and some court families later maintained it as a family crest. The Yoshino family adopted this motif because in the fixed poetic conventions of the Japanese it immediately called to mind the springtime slopes of Mt. Yoshino.

Despite the widespread popularity of the cherry blossom, its adoption as a family crest was unremarkable. Few warriors appear to have used this motif, and by any numerical count of family crests, the cherry blossom ranks surprisingly near the bottom.

274-75. Chestnut (*kuri*). The chestnut is more popular as a delicacy than as a design in Japan, although several families did use it as a family crest.

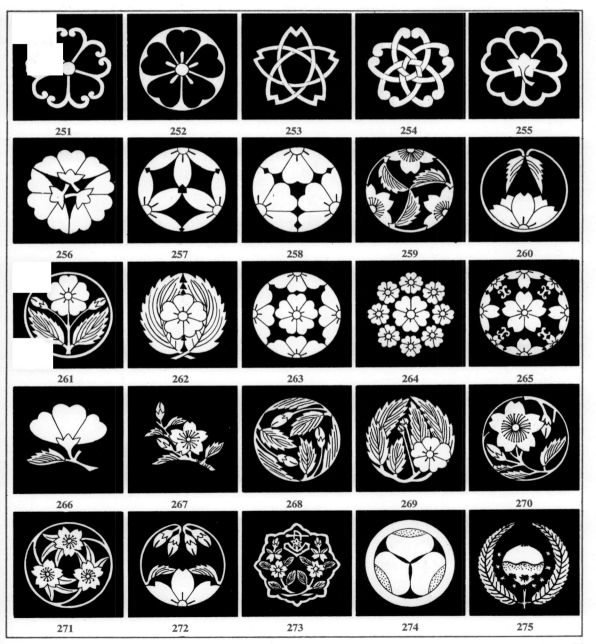

251 252 253 254 255
256 257 258 259 260
261 262 263 264 265
266 267 268 269 270
271 272 273 274 275

276-325. Chrysanthemum (*kiku*). The chrysanthemum plant was brought to Japan from T'ang China, and arrived with many of its legendary and superstitious connotations intact. Because of its ascribed nobility and purity, it was known as one of the "four princes" among subjects of art, the others being the plum blossom, bamboo, and orchid. Its resemblance to the sun led it to be called by alternative names such as "sun splendor" (*nikka*) and "sun spirit" (*nissei*)—and the depiction of the chrysanthemum-sun is in fact one of the most universal of ancient design motifs. In Chinese legend, the chrys-anthemum also became associated with long life, through tales of a class of mountain hermits who survived to hoary age by subsisting solely on a diet of this flower, and on this basis it was brewed as a medicinal tea from ancient times. Another of the epithets for chrysanthemum, *ennenso,* or "longevity plant," derives from this association. The crest of Kusunoki Masashige, the emperor Godaigo's masterful general, is a chrysanthemum-on-water associated with a variation on the Chinese legend telling of a mountain village so overgrown with chrys-anthemums that the blossoms floated on the mountain stream. The villagers, because they drank of these waters, rarely died before they reached a hundred years of age. The chrysanthemum festival celebrated in China from the time of the Han dynasty was reenacted annually in Japan on September 9, and on this occasion a special chrysanthemum wine was served, reflecting this same belief in the flower's beneficent properties. Like the blossoms of the cherry and plum, the chrysanthemum was also admired in Japan simply for its own intrinsic beauty, and chrysanthemum-viewing parties graced the autumn lives of the

276   277   278   279   280

281   282   283   284   285

286   287   288   289   290

291   292   293   294   295

296   297   298   299   300

extraordinarily aesthetic courtly class.

As a decorative pattern, the chrysanthemum became especially popular among the aristocracy in the late Heian period. Its close association with the imperial line, however, did not occur until the early thirteenth century, when the flamboyant emperor Gotoba took a special liking to the design and had it worked into his costumes and household items, and even engraved on his sword blades. A century later the emperor Godaigo, who displayed these emblems on his banners, gave certain loyal subjects the right to wear either the chrysanthemum or paulownia and with this the imperial association with the chrysanthemum became more or less formalized. Legislation concerning use of the chrysanthemum as a crest fluctuated with the fortunes of the imperial line, meaning that it was rarely taken seriously, and the chrysanthemum motif found fairly widespread use as a family emblem even outside of the immediate imperial family. It was, after all, auspicious, pretentious, and beautiful.

The selection given below is merely a part of the total number of variations which Japanese designers have developed on the chrysanthemum motif. The last two rows of crests (316-25) are all examples of the use of the chrysanthemum motif as an enclosure for other designs.

326-50. Clove (*choji*). In the Heian period, cloves were one of the exotic and costly items brought to Japan from Malacca and other distant lands and greatly prized by the upper class. Used to enhance both taste and status, the spice had other import as well. It was regarded as medicinally beneficial. It was also believed to bring good fortune when burned in the flame of a small lamp. As a pattern, the clove motif early became identified as one of the *takarazukushi*, a group of figures said to symbolize health, comfort, luxury, and the like. Several families used the motif as a family crest.

The selection below gives a good example of the double-design or double-motif convention common in Japanese crests. The clove becomes a paulownia (334), diamond (336–43), *tomoe* (343–47), *tomoe*-plum blossom (348), crane (349), and mother-and-child butterfly (350).

351-57. Clover (*hagi*). The *hagi*, or bush clover, is so closely identified with autumn in Japan that it is not only known as one of the "seven plants of autumn," but also written with a single ideograph literally meaning autumn-grass. In the classic eighth-century collection of poems, the *Man'yoshu*, the bush clover is

alluded to more frequently than either the plum or cherry blossoms. Its selection as a pattern lies entirely in its gracefulness.

358-60. Cosmus (*kosumusu*). The cosmus was foreign to Japan until recent times, and the designs below represent a turn-of-the-century attempt to treat this flower in the traditional style.

361-72. Cryptomeria (*sugi*). From earliest recorded times, the stately cryptomeria has been associated with various Shinto shrines in Japan, such as that of Miwa, and in many cases its adoption as a crest was based on such religious associations.

326 327 328 329 330
331 332 333 334 335
336 337 338 339 340
341 342 343 344 345
346 347 348 349 350

Since the needles of the cryptomeria remain green throughout the year, the tree—like its counterpart the pine—is also regarded as auspicious, a symbol of endurance. *Sugi* is also a familiar element in Japanese surnames, and families such as the Sugi, Uesugi, Sugida, and Sugiura selected the cryptomeria as a family crest for denotative purposes.

The last five cryptomeria designs below (368–72), some of which depict Shinto gateways and shrine gables, reveal the religious associations of the cryptomeria and also represent a more elaborate and realistic style of depiction more characteristic of Japanese painting and kimono design than of Japanese heraldry.

373-75. Dahlia (*dariya*). Like the cosmus, these designs represent a recent rendering of a flower which played little role in traditional Japanese design.

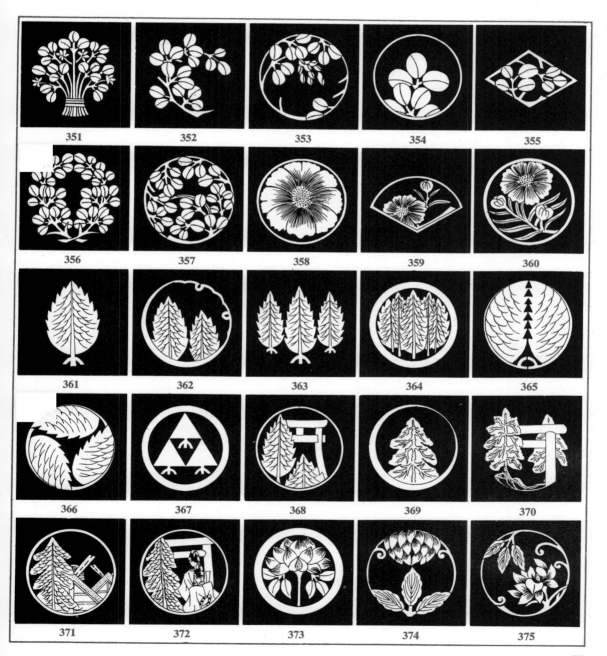

376-80. Eggplant (*nasu*). Originally of Indian origin, the eggplant is a common part of the Japanese diet. As a design motif, it was not used until the latter part of the feudal period.

381-85. Fern (*shida*). Formally identified as *Gleichenia longissima bl.*, the *shida*, described in an ancient saying as being "the color of spring," was used in New Year's ceremonies as part of an ancient Japanese folk practice, and thus carried auspicious connotations of growth and development.

386-87. Forsythia (*rengyo*). The forsythia was brought to Japan from China, and used for medicinal purposes. As a family crest, it was a rare and rather atypical design.

388-90. Gardenia (*kuchinashi*). The gardenia was used in both dyes and medicines in Japan, and first appeared as a design motif in the late feudal period.

391-410. Gentian (*rindo*). In early Japanese literature, the gentian was often used to convey a sense of autumnal loneliness. As a crest, it represents a good example of the type of pattern which became popular in the Heian period for purely decorative purposes, and then later was adopted as a formal family crest. The gentian crest is particularly associated with both the Seiwa and Murakami branches of the illustrious and powerful Minamoto (Genji) clan, and thus conveys to the Japanese a particularly aristocratic aura.

The basic rendering of the gentian (as seen below, 391–94) bears a striking resemblance to both the bamboo-leaf and paulownia designs. This was, of course, a deliberate artistic convention, but as the last designs in the selection reveal, Japanese draftsmen were capable of developing the gentian motif into complex and intricate patterns.

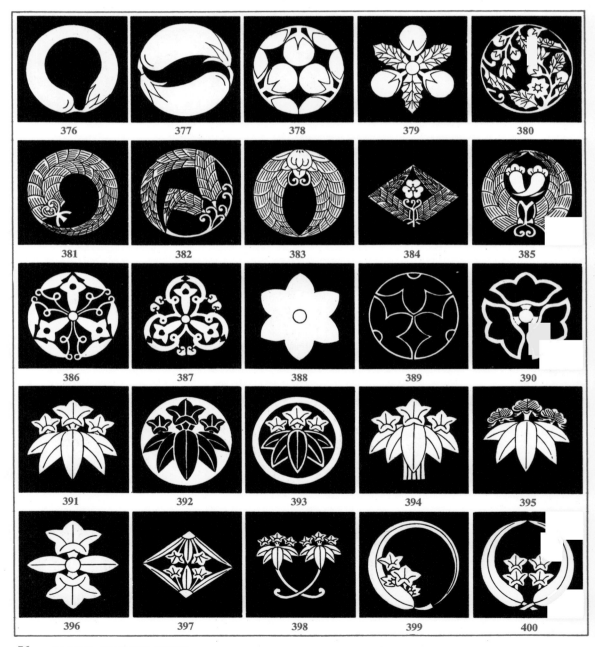

376   377   378   379   380
381   382   383   384   385
386   387   388   389   390
391   392   393   394   395
396   397   398   399   400

411-25. Gingko (*icho*). The gingko tree was brought to Japan from China at an early date, and was frequently planted on the grounds of temples and shrines. Thus, like the cryptomeria, it assumed religious connotations. In autumn the leaves of the tree turn yellow, and are greatly admired for their beauty. Probably because of this, the Japanese gingko pattern is based on the leaf of the tree and ignores the edible gingko nut, which is a delicacy in Japan. The shape of the leaf itself is aptly indicated in one of the several ways by which gingko can be rendered in classical Chinese: three ideo-graphs meaning "duck's-foot tree." By a rather torturous pun, the gingko is also said to have had a vaguely auspicious connotation, since by a homonym in the classical language it can also mean something along the lines of "barbarians bring tribute"— in other words, supremacy.

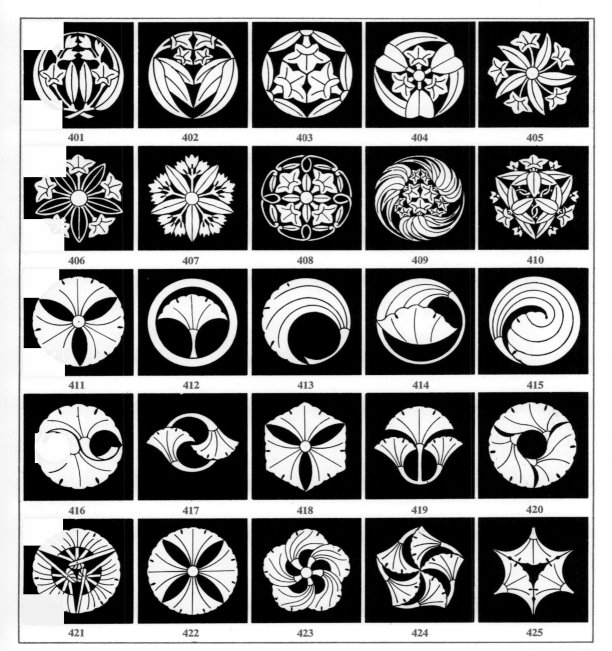

401 402 403 404 405

406 407 408 409 410

411 412 413 414 415

416 417 418 419 420

421 422 423 424 425

426-35. Gourd (*hyotan*). The gourd design did not appear until late in the feudal period, and never was adopted as a family crest. Its associations were probably too libertine to tie to the family name, for the gourd was best known as a dried and hollowed out container for carrying saké to festive occasions, as the last three designs suggest.

436-40. Grape (*budo*). The grape pattern was transmitted to Japan from the Asian continent during the Nara period. It was rarely associated with wine or inexpensive enlightenment in the Orient as it is in the West, and was admired for its beauty alone.

441-50. Hemp (*asanoha*). Often identified as one of the five basic crops or "grains" of ancient China, the hemp or flax plant played both sacred and profane roles in Japan. Not only was it used to make thread, rope, and cloth, but in early times in Japan it was also used to make the pendants (*nusa*) displayed at Shinto shrines. During the Heian period, hemp was also burned at the Bon Festival in midsummer to light departed spirits on their way.

451-60. Holly (*hiragi*). From at least as early as the Heian period until very recent times, holly was primarily associated with the exor-

cism of demons in Japan (see 459), being hung over the doorway while the exorcism ritual known as *tsuina* was performed (*see also* 726–33).

461-75. Hollyhock (*aoi*). Unlike many of the plants used as motifs in Japanese design, the hollyhock is native to Japan. At an undetermined date it became associated with the prestigious Kamo Shrine in Kyoto, and was adopted as the holy emblem of that institution. So close was the identification that Kyoto's renowned Kamo Festival, still held today, is formally known in Japanese as the Hollyhock Festival (*Aoi Matsuri*). Many families who favored this em

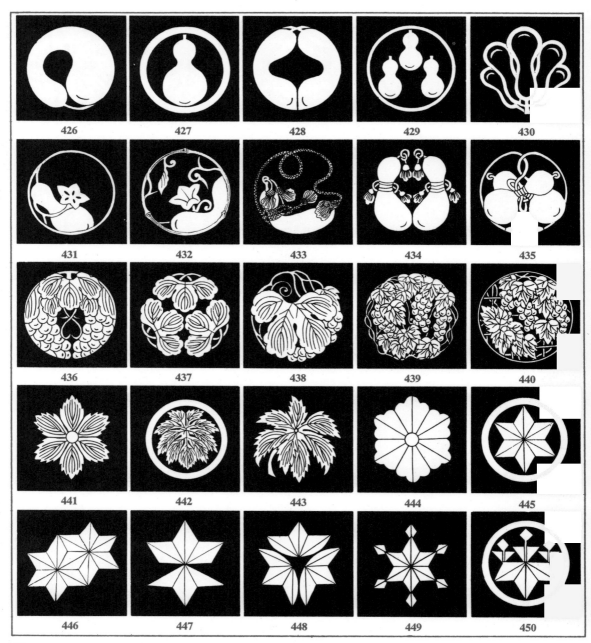

blem thus did so out of respect to this shrine or to the Tosho Shrine, also associated with the hollyhock.

The most illustrious bearer of the hollyhock as a family crest was one of the greatest bloodlines in Japanese history—the Tokugawa, who ruled the land for two-and-one-half centuries until Commodore Perry's visit toppled the old feudal edifice. Both the main shogunal line and branch families bearing the original clan name of Matsudaira used variations of the hollyhock as a family crest. A small number of loyal supporters of the Tokugawa were also granted the privilege of displaying this emblem.

Along with the chrysanthemum and paulownia, the hollyhock occupied the pinnacle of prestige among Japanese crests.

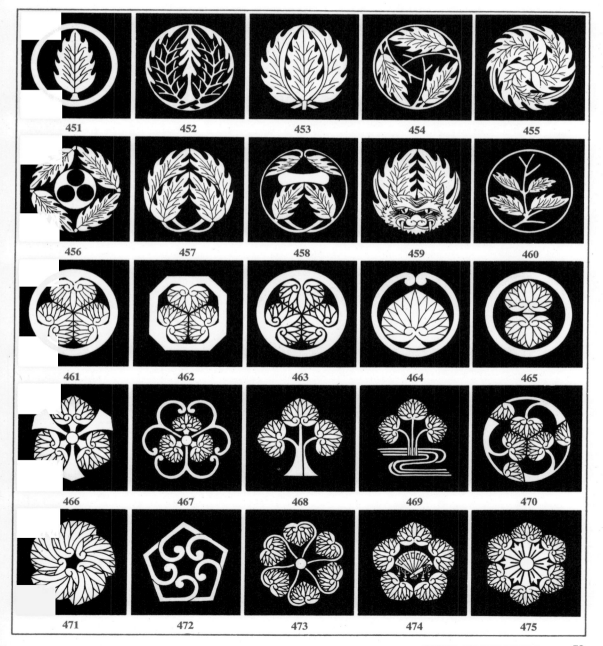

451 452 453 454 455

456 457 458 459 460

461 462 463 464 465

466 467 468 469 470

471 472 473 474 475

476-90. Iris (*kakitsubata*). A subject of poem and painting from early times in Japan, the iris received its most splendid and famous depiction in the folding screens painted by Ogata Korin in the early eighteenth century. During the Heian period, the Iris Festival was celebrated on the fifth day of the fifth month, and it was believed that at this time of year in particular, the fragrance of iris and mugwort would help to drive off evil spirits. As a design, the iris motif followed the familiar course of first appearing as a purely decorative device on the clothing and carriages of the court nobility and then later being adopted as a family crest in both court and warrior circles.

491-510. Ivy (*tsuta*). The *tsuta*, or Japanese ivy, ranks among the most popular motifs used in Japanese crests and provides a good sample of the various reasons why a particular motif might be adopted as a personal emblem. In early Japanese literature the ivy was praised for its beauty, and like other subjects such as the iris and chrysanthemum, it was first adopted as decoration on the costumes and furnishings of the aristocracy. Centuries later it assumed particular prestige because it was favored by eminent families such as some of the Matsudaira branches and the shogun Yoshimune himself. Eventually the ivy also attained special popularity as a crest among women of the pleasure quarters, who admired not only its gracefulness, but also its ability to survive and prosper by entwining itself around other bodies. Some families, such as the Tsutagi, adopted the ivy for denotative reasons. One possibly apocryphal story tells of a warrior family which adopted the ivy as a crest when its patriarch saved himself from a fatal fall into a crevice by seizing hold of a vine of ivy.

As a graphic design, the ivy bears fairly close resemblance to both the

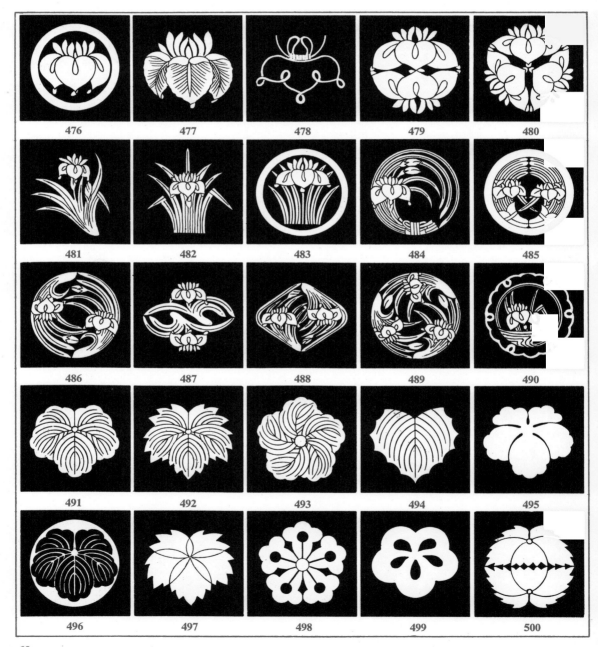

maple leaf and grape leaf. The selection below focuses particularly on the many variations possible with a frontal view of a single leaf.

511-12. Knotweed (*itadori*). A rare and abstracted version of a plant used in traditional medicine to stop pain.

513-25. Lily (*yuri; hiogi*). Two separate varieties are actually depicted below—the *yuri*, or ordinary lily (513–18), and the *hiogi*, sometimes defined as the leopard flower or blackberry lily (519–25). Neither was a traditional design motif in Japan.

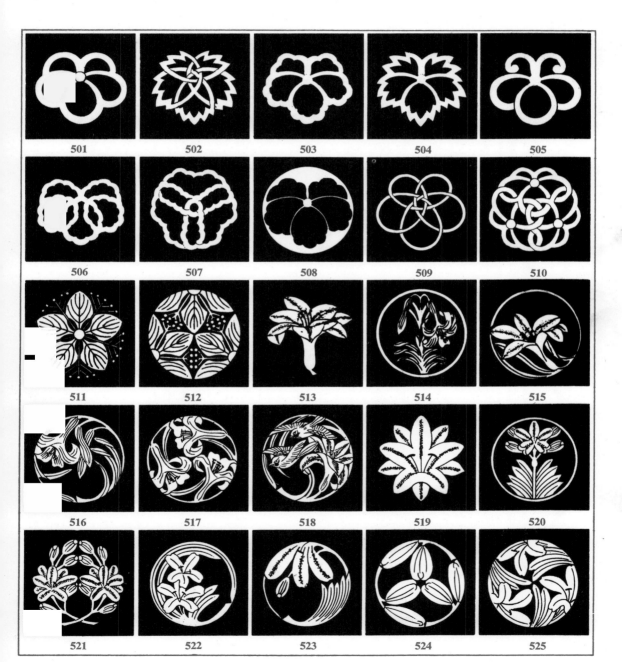

501

502

503

504

505

506

507

508

509

510

511

512

513

514

515

516

517

518

519

520

521

522

523

524

525

526-27. Loquat (*biwa*). In ancient times, the fruit of the loquat was served at the Boys' Festival on May 5, and the leaves had medicinal use. The musical instrument known as the *biwa* derives its name from its resemblance to the leaf of the loquat.

528-30. Lotus (*hasu*). Although the lotus is as much a symbol of Buddhism as the cross is of Christianity, symbolic of enlightenment, supreme truth, and of purity emerging from impurity, it appears surprisingly few times as a motif in Japanese heraldic design.

531-55. Mandarin Orange (*tachibana*). Reputedly brought to Japan from China in the third century A.D., the mandarin orange was immediately admired for its glossy green leaves, fragrant blossoms, and beautiful, succulent fruit. Traditionally, it was paired with the cherry tree before the Shishii-den (great ceremonial hall) of the imperial palace in Kyoto, and to the present day the two are displayed together among the formal dolls which each family with daughters puts out on the occasion of the Girls' Festival. As a family crest, the mandarin orange in its different versions was associated with the eminent Tachibana family, whose name was written with the same ideograph.

556-65. Maple Leaf (*kaede*). In a country which has made a cult of viewing natural objects of beauty, the autumn foliage-viewing ceremony quite naturally has its place among the various other festivities in which both ancient and modern Japanese have delighted. *Kaede*, the word for maple, is itself suggestive—the pronunciation puns on "frog's foot," which is how the ancients apparently described the leaf, while the single ideograph used is made up of the elements for tree and wind, conveying a rather gentle image of rustling foliage. Although the maple is celebrated in literature and appeared as

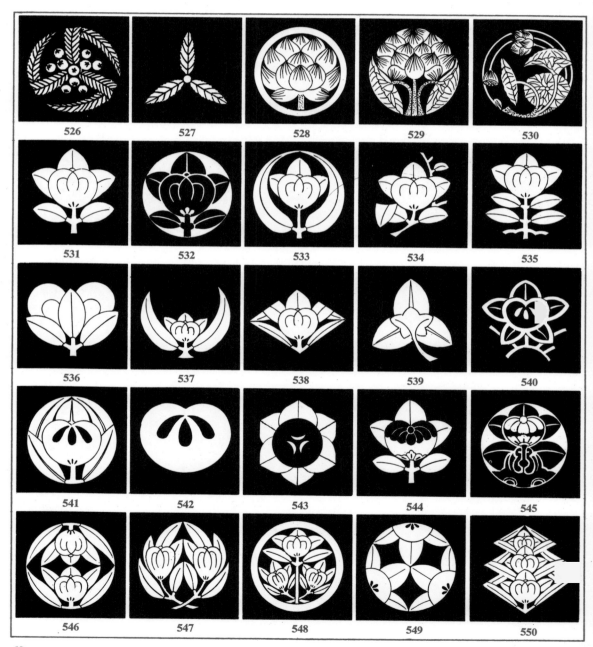

526 527 528 529 530
531 532 533 534 535
536 537 538 539 540
541 542 543 544 545
546 547 548 549 550

a decorative pattern before the feudal period, somewhat surprisingly—like the cherry blossom—it is not one of the more popular motifs among family crests.

566-67. Melon (*uri*). The decapitation of fallen foes was a common practice in feudal warfare as a means of making certain the identity of one's slain opponent, and medieval chronicles record an instance of a warrior who used the silhouette of a melon as a crest because this shape resembled the pool of blood which formed after he had performed this custom on the body of a particularly renowned foe.

A rare motif in this realistic depiction, the "melon" in abstract form was one of the most popular patterns in traditional Japanese graphics (*see 2401–25*).

568-70. Millet (*awa*). One of the "five grains" of ancient China, millet was brought to Japan in ancient times but was adapted as a pattern only in the late feudal period.

571-75. Mistletoe (*hoya*). The mistletoe was admired in ancient court society, and particularly praised as a textile design for its symmetry, but its primary association was with the Kanto area in eastern Japan, where the cream of the warrior class re-

sided. In particular, mistletoe was closely identified with the institutions devoted to worship of Hachiman, the god of war, and thus carried both religious and martial connotations. As a crest, it was frequently combined with pigeons, Hachiman's gentle messengers. (*see also 1376–85*).

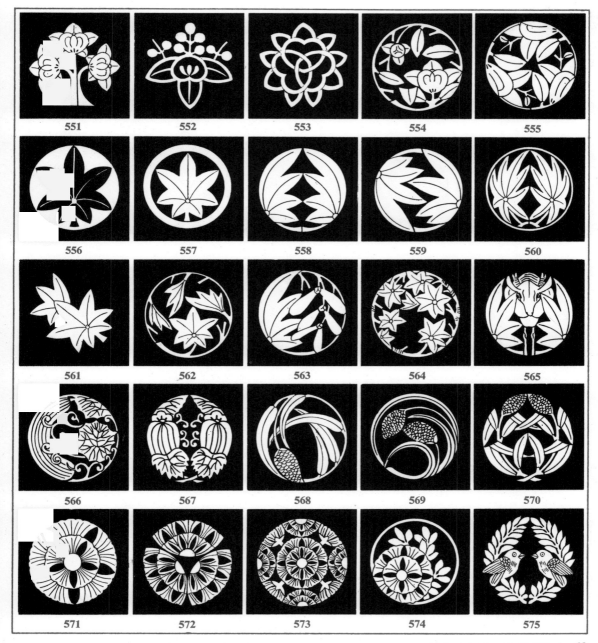

551 552 553 554 555

556 557 558 559 560

561 562 563 564 565

566 567 568 569 570

571 572 573 574 575

576-78. Moonflower (*yugao*). Literally "evening face," the white moonflower blooms in the evening, and was selected as a family crest by several families because of its beauty.

579-80. Morning Glory (*asagao*). The counterpart of the moonflower, *asagao* is the "morning face." It had little vogue as a design until the late feudal period.

581-90. Mulberry (*kaji*). In ancient times the leaf of the *kaji*, or "paper mulberry," was used to make receptacles for offerings of food at Shinto shrines, and clothing made of mulberry bark was also placed before the gods. The *gohei*, or paper strips,

still hung at Shinto shrines are said to symbolize this latter offering. In the late Heian period, court ladies used the leaf to write poems on when celebrating the Tanabata Festival. However, it was predominantly the religious associations of the mulberry which lay behind its fairly widespread adoption as a family emblem. Several shrines, including the Sumo Shrine, used it as their official emblem, and devout parishioners followed suit.

591-93. Nagi (*nagi*). Found clustered around both the Kasuga and Kumano shrines, the *nagi* tree had assumed such strong religious connotations by the Heian period that its

leaves were used as amulets and talismans. In the Izu Peninsula area it was believed to be efficacious in pacifying the seas, and in fact *nagi* is the same pronunciation for a different ideograph meaning lull or calm.

594-600. Nandin (*nanten*). A cultivated bush that grows as high as six to ten feet, the *nanten* is of the Japanese barberry family and puts forth a small red berry. It was adopted as a design in the late feudal period.

601-5. Narcissus (*suisen*). The natural wild and damp habitat of the narcissus is aptly indicated by its name in Japanese—*suisen*, literally "water hermit." Later cultivated in

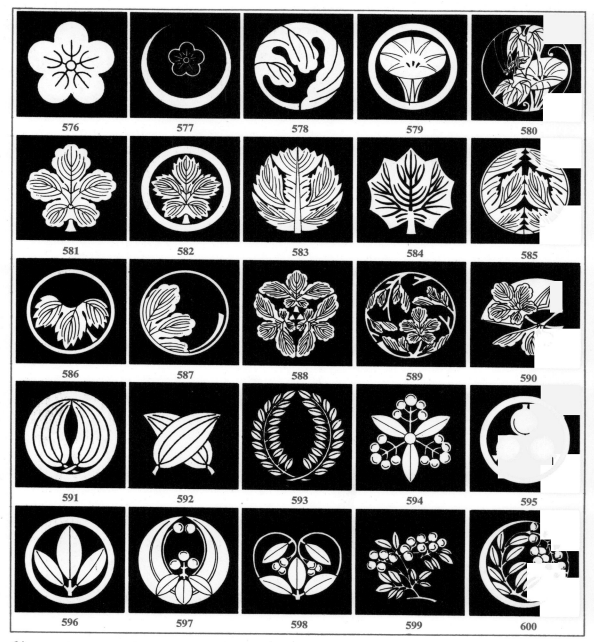

576   577   578   579   580

581   582   583   584   585

586   587   588   589   590

591   592   593   594   595

596   597   598   599   600

private gardens, this appeared as a crest only belatedly.

606-25. Oak (*kashiwa*). In both significance and appearance, the oak design bears a close resemblance to the mulberry. In very ancient times the oak leaf was used as a kind of dish on which to serve things, and from this it soon became associated with offerings to the gods. It was also associated with the Kumano, Kasuga, and Izu shrines. By the late Heian period the oak tree was regarded as the residence of the protective deities of forests and groves. This was one of the more popular crests among the warrior class, parti-

cularly among close devotees of Shinto. The oak leaf (*kaji-ba*) was used as a commemorative crest by the Matsura family of Kaji-tani (Oak Valley) in Hirado, a port town on an island off the coast of Kyushu.

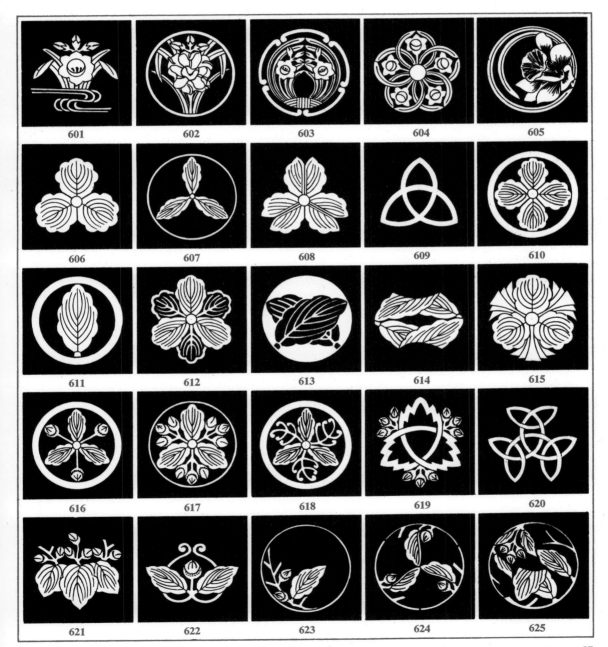

601 602 603 604 605

606 607 608 609 610

611 612 613 614 615

616 617 618 619 620

621 622 623 624 625

626-33. Orchid (*ran*). One of the "four princes" of Chinese painting, the orchid nonetheless failed to attain even middle-class status in Japanese heraldry, and was one of the more neglected design motifs. No family appears to have used it as a crest.

634-35. Paddy Plant (*denjiso*). Literally "paddy-ideograph plant," the *denjiso's* nomenclature is doubly appropriate. The plant itself takes root in shallow water and floats its leaves on the surface, while the four-petaled leaf depicted here is square-shaped like the ideograph for rice paddy.

636-45. Palm (*shuro*). As Sei Shonagon revealed in her *Pillow Book,* the *shuro,* or hemp palm, was prized by Heian aristocrats because of its exotic appearance. Graphically, the motif bears a close resemblance to the feather fan (*see* 1746–50).

646-52 Pampas Grass (*susuki*). One of the "seven plants of autumn," the pampas grass too was honored with viewing parties in ancient Japan. In the last two crests, the autumnal mood is captured in the flight of wild geese over the pampas grass. A kingfisher, a bird rarely depicted in Japanese design, also passes over the scene (650).

653-55. Pansy (*panji*). The designs below are modern renderings of a motif which played no role in Japanese heraldry.

656-75. Passion Flower (*tessen*). Selected as a crest by several noble families on the basis of its beauty alone, the passion flower is often planted in gardens among the bamboo. The inner disc of the blossom resembles a chrysanthemum, a likeness which Japanese draftsmen highlighted in many of their versions of this motif.

626	627	628	629	630
631	632	633	634	635
636	637	638	639	640
641	642	643	644	645
646	647	648	649	650

651

652

653

654

655

656

657

658

659

660

661

662

663

664

665

666

667

668

669

670

671

672

673

674

675

676-725. Paulownia (*kiri*). The most popular of all Japanese crests, the paulownia bears a heavy load of legendary and historic significance. According to Chinese legend, the mythical phoenix, bird of immortality, alights only in the branches of the paulownia tree when it comes to earth, and eats only the seed of the bamboo. Intricate depictions of the phoenix-paulownia-bamboo were worked into Chinese textiles on the basis of this legend; occasionally a fourth element, the unicorn, was added. The unicorn was not developed as a theme in Japanese design, but the other three were taken over intact and displayed on the Japanese imperial robes at an early date. They soon came to be used independently as designs, and by the late Heian and Kamakura periods, the paulownia pattern had become extremely fashionable throughout the entire aristocracy.

As an explicitly imperial crest, the paulownia ranks only slightly behind the chrysanthemum, and both are usually taken as the dual emblems of the Japanese throne. This association developed gradually, and was formalized only in the early thirteenth century, when the emperor Godaigo conferred both the chrysanthemum and paulownia crests upon Ashikaga Takauji, founder of the Ashikaga line of shoguns, who held nominal military control over Japan for the next century and a half. While maintaining their original family crest of two parallel lines, the Ashikaga shoguns, beginning with Takauji himself, proceeded to use the paulownia as a mark of favor of their own. A number of powerful daimyo who gave their support to the Ashikaga were rewarded with the right to wear the prestigious paulownia, and from this time on the paulownia crests conveyed a heady aura of both legitimacy and power.

In the late sixteenth century the brilliant and maverick Toyotomi Hideyoshi clamped his control over the land and was granted use of the paulownia by the throne itself. A commoner by birth, Hideyoshi used this as his own family crest, and had it emblazoned, engraved, embossed, and incised on all of the monumental construction projects he sponsored around Osaka and Kyoto. With even greater munificence than the Ashikaga before him, Hideyoshi also granted use of the paulownia crest to the most loyal of his lieutenants. By the late feudal period, so many families had come to use the pau-

lownia through conferral, inheritance, or subterfuge that a weary phoenix would have been able to alight on nearly one-fifth of the warrior population of Japan.

As the selection below indicates, an almost infinite variety of renderings was possible by altering the style of either the leaf or blossoms of the paulownia.

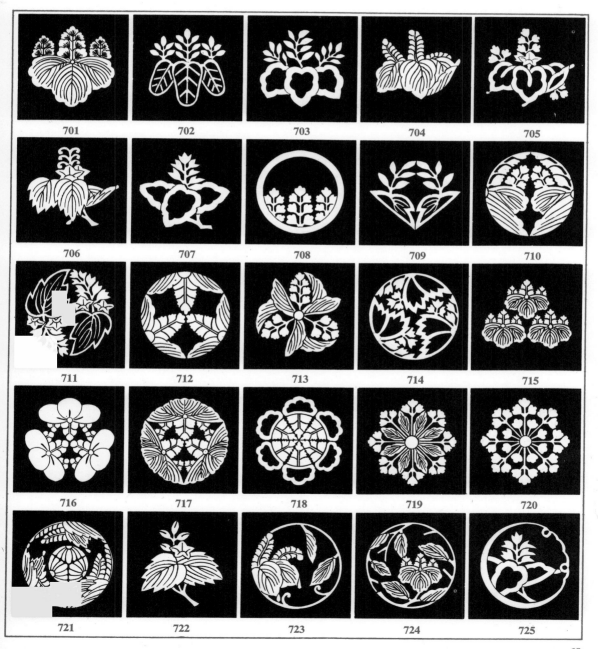

701 702 703 704 705
706 707 708 709 710
711 712 713 714 715
716 717 718 719 720
721 722 723 724 725

726-33. Peach (*momo*). In Chinese poetry the beauty and freshness of a young girl is likened to a peach, but as a crest motif the peach was probably chosen as much for its auspicious connotations as for its aesthetic appeal. In China, the peach was associated with exorcism, and in Japanese mythology the god Izanagi is reputed to have driven off devils with the same fruit. This association was symbolized in the *tsuina* ceremony in which a bow made from the wood of the peach tree was used to "shoot" evil spirits. Generally the fruit itself is drawn, but the last crest below (733) depicts the blossom.

734-40. Pear (*nashi*). Sometimes called "Chinese pear" (*karanashi*) or "pear cross-section" (*nashi kiriguchi*), this is one of the more misleading motifs. In all probability the design existed before the "pear" label was assigned to it. The last designs (739–40) depict the blossom of the pear.

741-70. Peony (*botan*). Known as "the sovereign of the flowers" in China, the peony was brought from that country to Japan, where it was both admired for its beauty and used in traditional medicine. First as a decorative pattern and later as a family crest, the peony ranked almost as

high as the chrysanthemum, paulownia and hollyhock in prestige. In particular, it was associated with the aristocratic Konoe and Takatsukasa lines, as well as being adopted as the emblem of several influential temples and shrines.

771-73. Pepper (*togarashi*). A late and rare motif, the pepper's etymology is more interesting than its aesthetics. Literally and colorfully, the two ideographs with which it is written mean "China tartness."

774-75. Persimmon (*kaki*). Although the spectacle of deep-orange persimmon heavy on the bough is one of Japan's great visual delights—

726   727   728   729   730
731   732   733   734   735
736   737   738   739   740
741   742   743   744   745
746   747   748   749   750

and although it is customary to offer persimmon to the gods at the New Year—this remains one of the inexplicably neglected motifs in Japanese design.

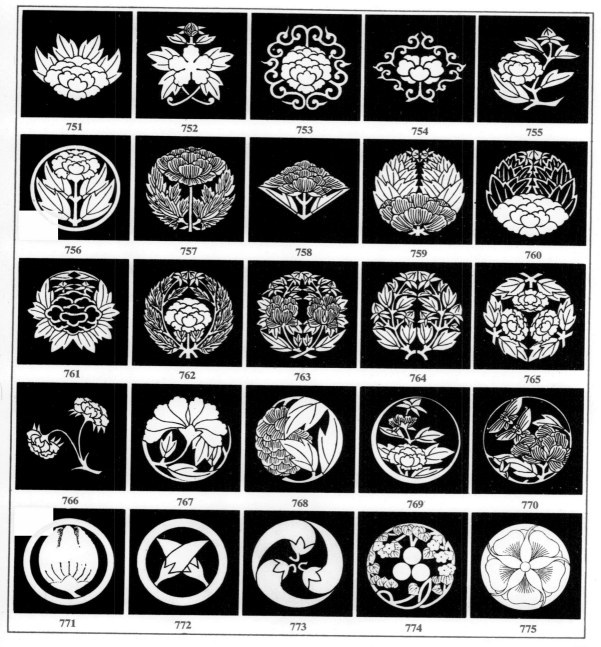

751	752	753	754	755
756	757	758	759	760
761	762	763	764	765
766	767	768	769	770
771	772	773	774	775

776-820. Pine (*matsu*). Green through all seasons, the pine—like the chrysanthemum, tortoise, and crane—was an auspicious sign of longevity, symbolizing a thousand years of life. Resistant to the wind, resilient beneath the snow, it joined the bamboo and early-blooming plum blossom as one of the "three companions of the deep cold" of Chinese tradition. At New Year's in Japan, pine branches are attached over the door or gateway of the house. In addition to these desirable associations and the fact that it lent itself to graceful designs, the pine also was popular as a crest for denotative reasons. Families such as the Matsuo, Akamatsu, Matsuda, and Matsumura adopted the pine motif for this reason.

The selection below indicates the several subsections of the general pine-motif category: stylized old pine trees (776–90), branch-and-needle clusters (791–96), pine cones (797–800), and pine-needle patterns (800–820). The latter are a particularly good example of combined or overlapping motifs in Japanese design, for there the pine needles are also: paulownia (800), diamonds (801–2); hollyhock (803); the ideograph *dai*, or "great," repeated three times (804); a circular "ball rack" (805; *see* 2231–35); cherry blossom (806); pinwheel or windmill (807); wood sorrel (808); sails (809); *tomoe* (810); crane (811); and butterfly (812). The last selections in this category (813–20) are all differently styled enclosures drawn with pine needles.

821-25. Pink (*nadeshiko*). Both the wild and domestic varieties of pink are found in Japan, but it is the former, distinguished by more jagged petal tips, which provides the motif used in Japanese patterns and crests.

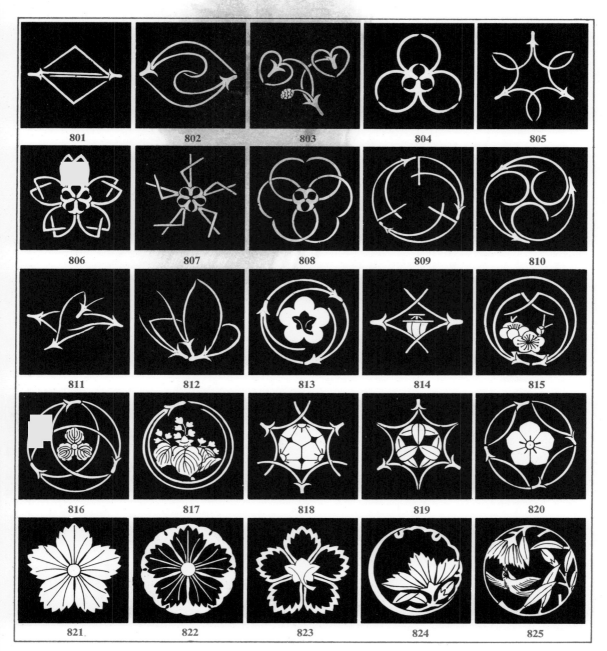

801   802   803   804   805

806   807   808   809   810

811   812   813   814   815

816   817   818   819   820

821   822   823   824   825

826-35. Plantain (*basho; obako*). Two different varieties are embraced here. The *basho* tree (826–33) bears a small banana-like fruit and is most famous in Japanese culture for having provided the sobriquet to the greatest of all haiku poets, Basho, who resided in a small hut beside such a plantain. The *obako* plant (834–35) was best known for its medicinal use. As crests, both were introduced late in the feudal period.

836-900. Plum Blossom (*ume*). The plum blossom represents more than beauty in the Orient. Delicate and fragile, it nonetheless appears early in the year, impervious to lingering winter chills, and thus takes a brave place alongside the bamboo and pine as one of the East's traditional "three companions of the deep cold." Much of a practical nature was also associated with the plum blossom. Its fruit was edible, and used medicinally as well. Dyestuffs were made from the blossoms of the brilliant red-blossomed variety. In Japan, the plum blossom also had both religious and commemorative associations.

Chinese poets had long extolled the plum blossom, and Japanese versifiers initially followed suit; in the eighth-century anthology, the *Man'yoshu,* the blossom of the plum is alluded to more than twice as frequently as that of the cherry. Early Japanese chronicles speak of plum-blossom-viewing festivities in Japan as early as A.D. 730, and as a textile design the plum blossom was already a popular motif in the Nara period. The plum-blossom pattern was particularly fashionable in the early Heian period, when it was displayed on clothing, furnishings, carriages, and especially on the backs of mirrors. In some of its versions, as is clear in the designs below, the plum-blossom design tended to become virtually indistinguishable from the depiction of six circular stars.

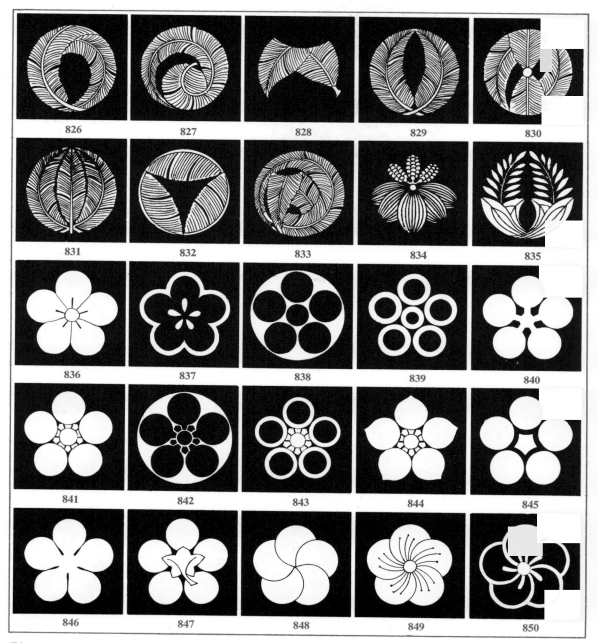

As the T'ang dynasty collapsed and Chinese influence on Japanese culture waned, the plum blossom tended to decline in favor in Japan and become replaced by the native cherry blossom. This transition was vividly exemplified in the year 960 when a fire ravaged the imperial palace, destroying a famous plum tree by its entrance; when the palace was reconstructed, a cherry tree was planted in the plum tree's stead. Despite this chill breath of nativism, however, as a decorative pattern the plum blossom remained true to its tradition of endurance and emerged as one of the more popular motifs in Japanese heraldry. To a large extent, this was due to the fact that it was known to have been admired by Sugawara Michizane, a late ninth-century courtier of such heroic accomplishments that he was posthumously deified as Tenjin, patron god of poetry, calligraphy, scholarship, and the like. The Temman Shrine, associated with worship of Tenjin, adopted the plum blossom as its official crest, and during the later centuries when Japanese heraldry was in flower, many families adopted the plum blossom as their family crest either to commemorate a lineage tracing back to Michizane or to signify their religious devotion to Temmangu.

The selection presented here is a good although incomplete sample of the Japanese draftsman's gift for variation on a theme. Many of these variations also serve as examples of the strikingly bold and modern dimension of much of traditional Japanese heraldic design. The patterns at the end of the selection show a development away from more simple emblematic design toward the complex renderings associated with kimono design. In addition to such conventional contortions as crane (873) and butterfly (874–75), some

unusual variations are also introduced: a blossom with auspicious "abalone strips" (866; *see* 1651–70); tiny, stylized wild geese between the petals of a bloom (885); and blossoms lying on a packet of incense (900). The popular convention of introducing a sword blade among the petals was also widely practiced with the plum-blossom motif.

901-02. Pomegranate (*zakuro*). This lush design was introduced in fairly recent times and played no role in traditional Japanese heraldry.

903-07. Poppy (*hinageshi*). Of foreign origin, neither the poppy nor opium played a significant role

in premodern Japan, and this motif, like that of the pomegranate, is a recent one. By an alternative version, the poppy is known as *bijinso*, or "beautiful woman plant."

908-10. Radish (*daikon*). One of the "seven plants of spring," the giant white radish has numerous superstitious and religious connotations. By a far-fetched pun on the classical language, it can be called *raifuku*, or "come fortune." In ancient religious ceremonies it was associated with parsley and shepherd's purse as a particularly auspicious food for certain occasions. In esoteric Buddhism, a forked radish was

the symbol of Shoten (Vinayaksha), the elephant-headed god, and this obvious fertility symbolism came to bode prosperity and success.

911-20. Reed (*ashi*). A famous line in the eighth-century *Nihon Shoki* chronicle described Japan as "land of the reedy plains," and in the Heian period this provided the motif for a popular pattern used especially on writing paper.

Rice Plant (*ine*). Rice, Asia's staff of life, had obvious auspicious and religious connotations. From early times, it was used as an offering to the gods, and the bound sheafs depicted below suggest this

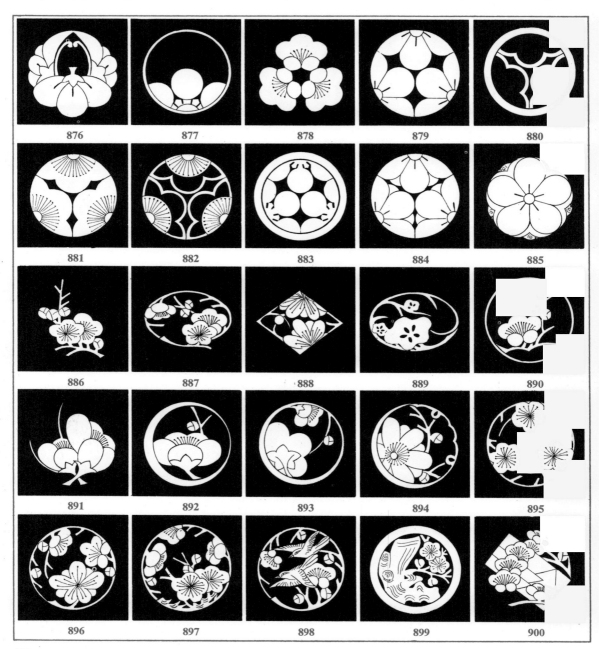

876 877 878 879 880
881 882 883 884 885
886 887 888 889 890
891 892 893 894 895
896 897 898 899 900

association. As a family crest, the rice plant also served as a denotative emblem for a wide variety of surnames which included ideographs meaning such things as rice plant, rice, paddy, unhulled rice, and the like. One of the best-known families which used the rice-plant crest was the Suzuki of Kii (present Wakayama and Mie prefectures), whose surname allegedly meant "piling up ears of rice" in the ancient dialect of that locale. The Kumano Shrine, also in Kii, became associated with the emblem of the rice plant, and some families later used the same motif as their crest to signify their reverence.

The selection here includes several rice-plant enclosures (936–42), concluding with a free-wheeling design combining sparrows, *tomoe,* and a sheaf of rice.

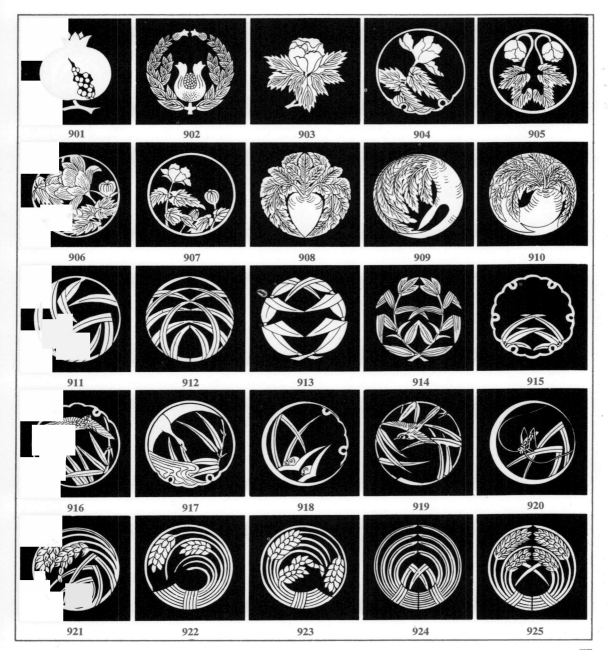

943-47. Rose (*bara*). This design, like the flower itself, was probably introduced to Japan only in the early modern period.

948-50. Shepherd's Purse (*nazuna*). Associated with radish and parsley as an "auspicious food," the shepherd's purse also had wide medical application in premodern Japan. Since its leaves were thought to resemble the plectrum of a samisen, it was sometimes called, onomatopoetically, the *pen-pen* plant (*pen-pengusa*).

951-62. Spatterdock (*kohone*). Although the spatterdock bears a large yellow flower, crests based on this motif depict the leaf—primarily, it appears, because of its close resemblance to the prestigious hollyhock.

963-75. Tea Berry (*chanomi*). Tea was introduced into Japan from China by Saicho, founder of the Tendai sect of Buddhism, at the beginning of the ninth century. For several centuries, however, it remained in use primarily for medicinal purposes, and it was not until the Zen monk Eisai "reintroduced" tea in the twelfth century that it began to be appreciated as a social and ceremonial beverage. The origin of the tea berry design is obscure, but it appears to have been derived from the already well-established design based on the mandarin orange; the latter differs from the former in that it has three leaves behind the fruit and a small circle near the top of the fruit. The relationship between the tea berry and mandarin orange designs is similar to that between the spatterdock and hollyhock, or between the zingiber and tassel (*see* 1106–50 and 2081–90).

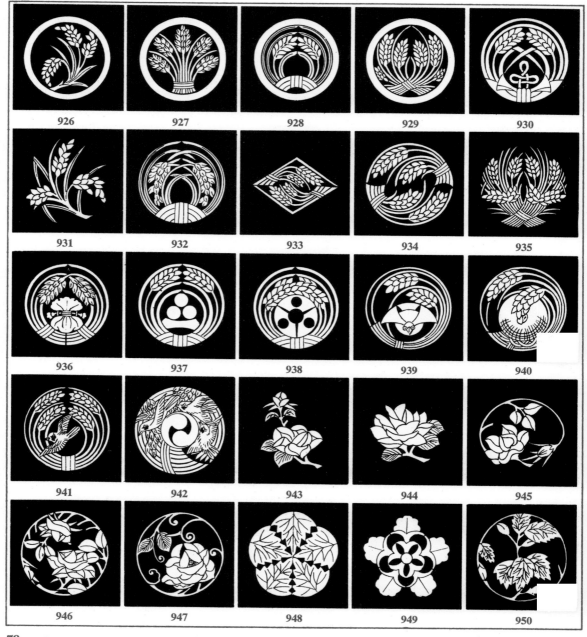

926 927 928 929 930
931 932 933 934 935
936 937 938 939 940
941 942 943 944 945
946 947 948 949 950

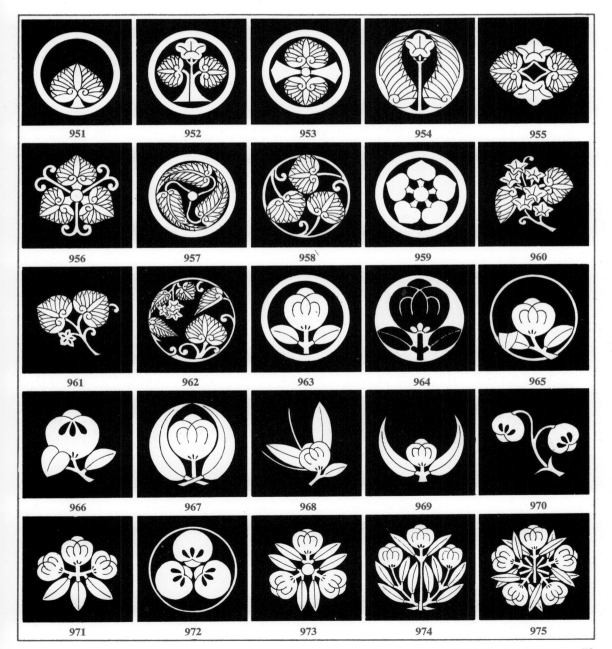

951   952   953   954   955

956   957   958   959   960

961   962   963   964   965

966   967   968   969   970

971   972   973   974   975

976-78. Tulip (*churippu*). Both flower and design were introduced into Japan in recent times.

979-80. Turnip (*kabu*). Although its significance is not clear, the turnip appears to have been ascribed quasi-magical properties similar to those associated with parsley, radish, and the like.

981-85. Violet (*sumire*). A comparatively rare motif, the violet was nonetheless adopted as a family crest by one daimyo in the late feudal period. The last design (985) is a modern version.

986-90. Walnut (*kurumi*). The walnut, or "barbarian peach" as its ideographs read if taken literally, was adopted as a crest motif only in the late feudal period.

991-1025. Water Plantain (*omodaka*). Patterns based on the leaf and flowers of the water plantain appear to have become fashionable in the latter part of the Heian period, largely because the unusual shape of the leaf struck a popular chord of fancy. From the very beginning of the feudal period, even before the widespread adoption of family crests, many warriors displayed the design on their robes and armor—possibly because one of the plant's alternative names was *shogunso,* or "victory plant." With the adoption of formal crests by the warriors, this vogue increased, and by the end of the Edo period the water plantain was widely used as a family crest.

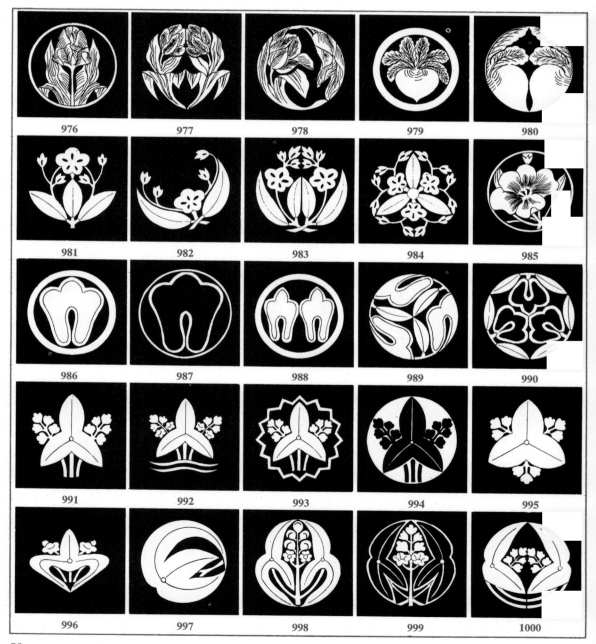

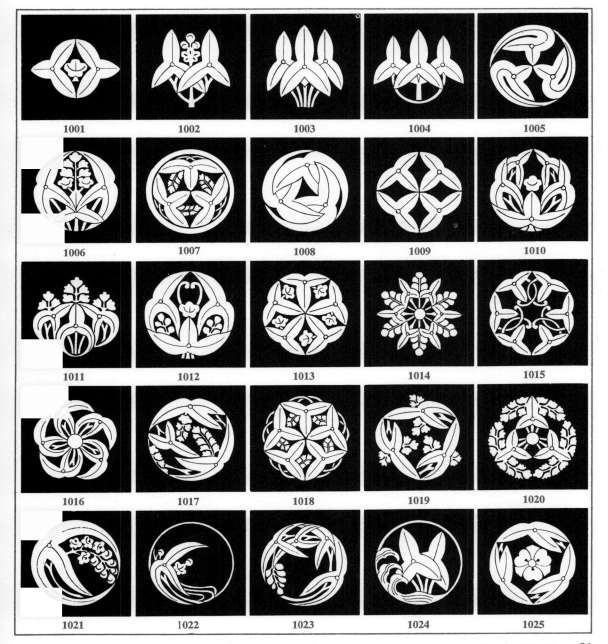

1001   1002   1003   1004   1005

1006   1007   1008   1009   1010

1011   1012   1013   1014   1015

1016   1017   1018   1019   1020

1021   1022   1023   1024   1025

1026-75. Wisteria (*fuji*). The wisteria is found growing wild in the Kansai (Kyoto-Osaka) area of Japan, and as allusions in the *Man'yoshu* reveal, it was already singled out for admiration in the Nara period. Eventually it was domesticated and trained to grow on arbors and trellises, with clusters of soft purple flowers trailing down from overhead to create a lovely and fragrant bower. The first wisteria-viewing parties were not held until the reign of the emperor Daigo (897–930), however, and the real vogue of the wisteria did not occur until the apogee of Fujiwara power in the latter half of the Heian period. Transcribed literally, the Fujiwara surname means "field of wisteria," and in both their textile and landscape design, the clan made prominent display of the wisteria. Despite this natural association, however, Japanese genealogies reveal that in later centuries only a small percentage of the families descended from this greatest of Japanese aristocratic lineages actually used the wisteria as their main family crest. Families with "fuji" as part of their name sometimes combined calligraphy and design, as in the crest of the Kato family (1058), where the character for *ka* was enclosed in a circular wisteria pattern (*to* is the Chinese reading for wisteria). Families expressing devotion to the Kumano Shrine also used wisteria, one of the plants associated with it. As the selections below reveal, it is certainly one of the most graceful and intricate of the traditional Japanese design motifs.

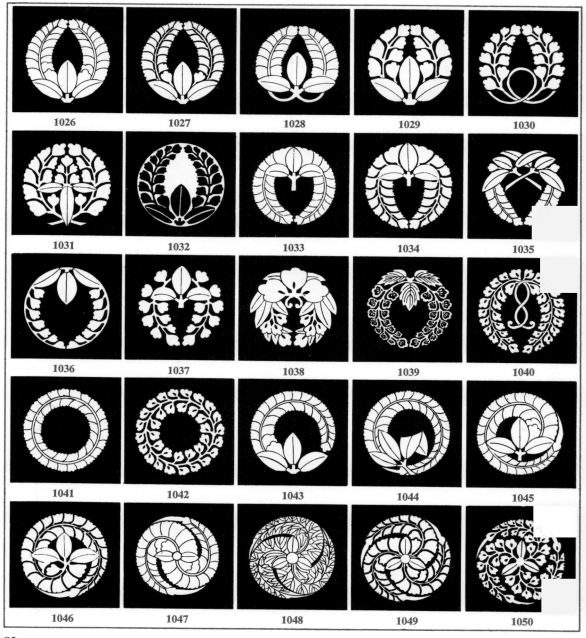

1026 1027 1028 1029 1030
1031 1032 1033 1034 1035
1036 1037 1038 1039 1040
1041 1042 1043 1044 1045
1046 1047 1048 1049 1050

1051   1052   1053   1054   1055

1056   1057   1058   1059   1060

1061   1062   1063   1064   1065

1066   1067   1068   1069   1070

1071   1072   1073   1074   1075

1076-1100. Wood Sorrel (*kata-bami*). In early days in Japan, the leaf of the wood sorrel was used to make a medicinal salve, and also to polish bronze mirrors; because of the latter use, it was also known as *kagami-gusa* or "mirror plant." Although the wood sorrel produces a small five-petaled flower, patterns and crests based on this plant invariably depict the trifoliate clover-like leaf rather than the flower. This pattern was particularly popular as a decoration on carriages in the Heian period, and later came to enjoy a tremendous vogue among the warrior class for various reasons.

The fruit of the wood sorrel contains many seeds, and the plant is extremely reproductive. In later centuries, some warriors who used the wood sorrel as an emblem cited this characteristic as an auspicious token for the future proliferation of their families. Of greater appeal to the martial class than this tenuous implication, however, was the graphic convention of introducing a sword-blade device into the depiction of the leaf itself. For some reason, as the selection below indicates, this convention was particularly widely practiced in drawing the wood sorrel; if blades were not inserted between

each leaf, then at the very least the small tuck at the base of each leaf was depicted as a tiny blade. Even the wood-sorrel butterfly (1099) bristles at the beholder.

1101-05. Yamabuki (*yamabuki*). The *yamabuki,* sometimes called "yellow rose" in English, grows by the waterside and is often found as a pattern on the back of bronze mirrors of the Heian period. One Japanese family adopted this motif as their family crest because the native place of their progenitor was famous for its profusion of *yamabuki*—a rather classic example of a family crest commemorating locale.

1076 1077 1078 1079 1080
1081 1082 1083 1084 1085
1086 1087 1088 1089 1090
1091 1092 1093 1094 1095
1096 1097 1098 1099 1100

1106-50. Zingiber (*myoga*). Just as the tea-berry design derived from the mandarin orange and then assumed an identity and associations of its own, so the zingiber actually appears to be a variant of an earlier design depicting a horse's tassel (*see* 2081–90). In some instances, the two designs are virtually indistinguishable, but as a general rule the zingiber has veins on the leaf, while the tassel sports a small semicircular embellishment resembling a sunburst. In popularity, the derivative zingiber motif below eventually outstripped the parent design.

One major reason for the popularity of the zingiber association was undoubtedly the fact that it permitted a most auspicious pun, for written with different ideographs, *myoga* also means "divine protection." In the period of high feudalism, the zingiber crest also became associated with certain Buddhist temples and gods, thus adding a more solidly religious dimension to the motif; this was, of course, the very era when feudal strife was most fierce and divine assistance of whatever kind most greatly appreciated.

In the last designs below, the small flower that tops the zingiber emerges to take on a rather entomological existence of its own, although Japanese genealogies identify this version of the motif simply as "the flower of the *myoga*."

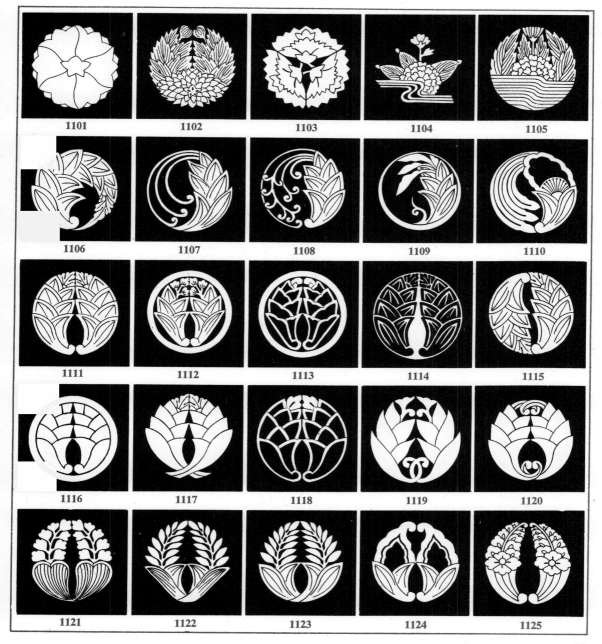

1126 1127 1128 1129 1130
1131 1132 1133 1134 1135
1136 1137 1138 1139 1140
1141 1142 1143 1144 1145
1146 1147 1148 1149 1150

Birds, Beasts, and Insects

1151-65. Antlers and Horns (*tsuno*). Deer antlers (*shikatsuno*, 1151–61) and other horns (*fukurotsuno*, 1162–65) appear to have been chosen as design motifs primarily for their symmetry rather than any larger connotations. During the height of feudal warfare, however, such objects acquired a martial implication, since decorative horns and antlers were often affixed to battle helmets (*see* 1827). One family had a commemorative crest of antlers to express pride in the physical strength of one of their men who had torn the antlers from the head of a deer with his bare hands.

1166-70. Bat (*komori*). The second ideograph in the word for bat (*mori*) can also be read *fuku*—and *fuku* in turn can be written with an ideograph meaning "good fortune." By such an etymological contortion, even the unlovely bat becomes an auspicious omen in Japan. The last two of the creatures depicted below are doubly benign, for they are formed out of an oak leaf and a paulownia leaf respectively.

1171-1215. Butterfly (*cho*). The butterfly pattern was a favorite among Japanese aristocrats as early as the Nara period, and appears to have been favored almost exclusively for its elegance. Even before the period of Japanese heraldry, warriors frequently displayed this pattern on their armor, and—perhaps revealingly—men of the ill-fated Taira (Heike) clan were known to be particularly fond of the butterfly design. During the period of high feudalism, when bloodletting reached a peak in Japan, the docile butterfly somewhat paradoxically enjoyed great popularity among upstart warriors selecting a family crest for the first time. To a large extent, this symbolized the other side of the warrior's harsh life —his susceptibility to the effete graces of the courtly society. The

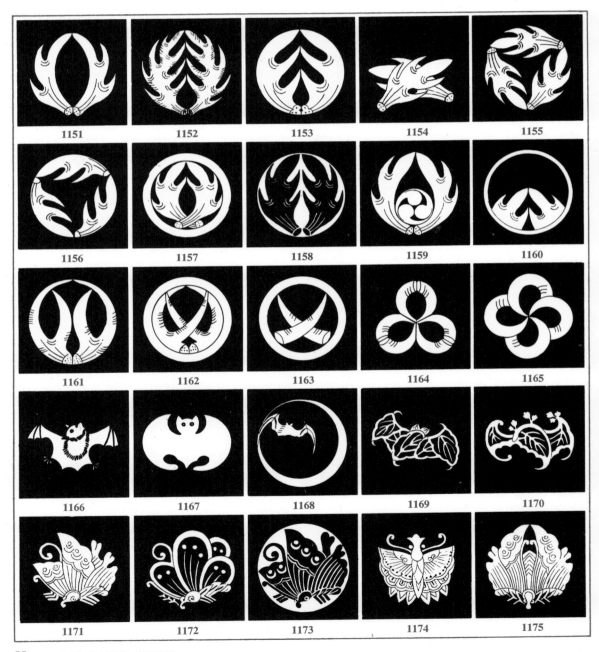

Okochi family used the flying butterfly (*fusencho*) as a crest to commemorate their native place, Fusencho in Mikawa (present Aichi Prefecture). Among designs based on living creatures, the butterfly motif enjoyed by far the greatest popularity.

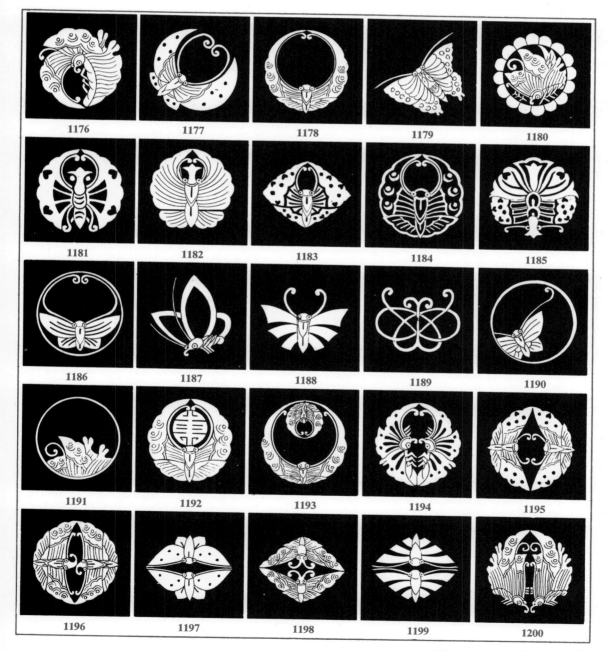

1176	1177	1178	1179	1180
1181	1182	1183	1184	1185
1186	1187	1188	1189	1190
1191	1192	1193	1194	1195
1196	1197	1198	1199	1200

1216-20. Centipede (*mukade*). Among the four Buddhist guardians, protectors of the four directions, the centipede is regarded as the "vassal" of Tamonten, guardian of the north. Although the emblem is used on certain festival days in Japan, it does not appear as a formal family crest.

1221-25. Crab (*kani*). A few warrior families used the crab motif as a family crest, apparently because of the martial significance of the crab's "armor" and alert defensive posture.

1226-62. Crane (*tsuru*). Both in its natural habitat and as a subject of literature or design, the crane was associated with the pine, bamboo, and tortoise, and prized for its auspicious connotations, symbolizing a thousand years of life. According to Chinese and Japanese legend, hermit-sages rode on cranes. Like the other items mentioned above, the crane also appeared as a decorative element during the Heian period, and was often applied to the backs of mirrors. Some families bearing the surnames Tsuru and Tsuruda adopted the crane as a denotative family crest. Although an elegant and elaborate design originally associated with the court, the crane, like the butterfly, proved popular as a family crest among the warrior class. A design of two cranes facing each other was used by the Nambu family to commemorate their victory over the Akita, when two of these auspicious birds suddenly dropped from the sky and alighted in the Nambu encampment on the eve of the battle.

Several highly different styles are revealed in the Japanese designs based on the crane. The last five designs below depict the crane made with Japanese *origami* (folding paper).

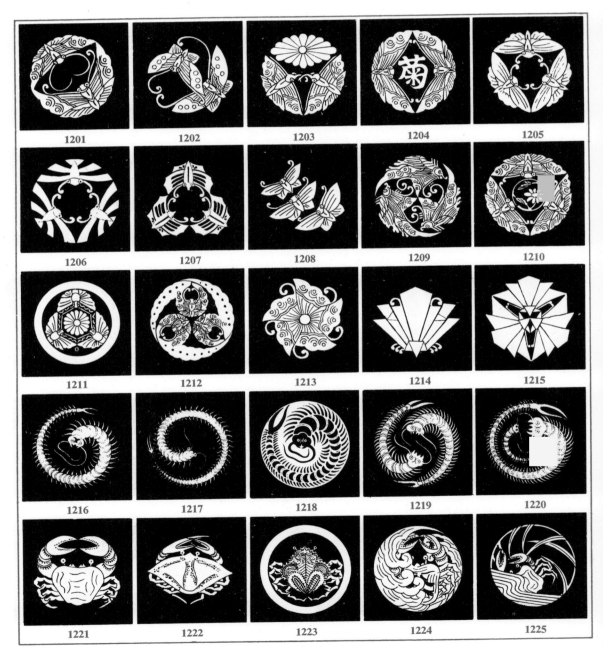

1201 1202 1203 1204 1205
1206 1207 1208 1209 1210
1211 1212 1213 1214 1215
1216 1217 1218 1219 1220
1221 1222 1223 1224 1225

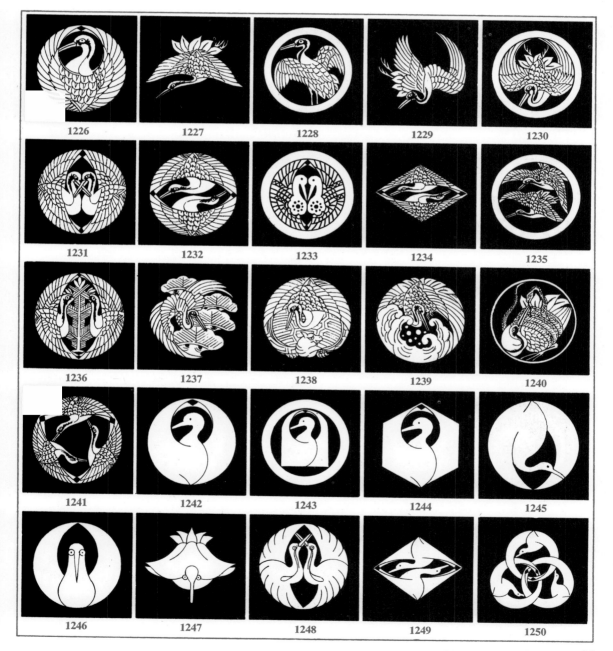

1226

1227

1228

1229

1230

1231

1232

1233

1234

1235

1236

1237

1238

1239

1240

1241

1242

1243

1244

1245

1246

1247

1248

1249

1250

1263-65. Crow (*karasu*). In Chinese and Japanese mythology, the crow is associated with the sun. Jimmu, Japan's semilegendary first emperor, was visited by such a divine bird during his migration from Kyushu to the Yamato (present Nara Prefecture) area. In later centuries, the crow became the sacred envoy of Kumano Shrine, and because of this association, several parishioners adopted it as a family crest. Traditional Japanese versions of the crow are hardly distinguishable from renderings of other birds such as the pigeon.

1266-68. Cuckoo (*hototogisu*). A subject of poetry but not of heraldry in Japan, the designs below are early twentieth-century versions of a bird traditionally admired for its song.

1969-70. Deer (*shika*). Although the deer appears in early Japanese poetry and design, and became closely associated with Kasuga Shrine in Nara, only the antlers of the animal actually made their way into the formal heraldry of Japan (*see* 1151–65). The designs below, both deer with cryptomeria, are fairly recent versions.

1271-83. Demon (*oni*). Japanese books of heraldry never classify the demon separately, although it frequently appears in conjunction with other motifs such as the peony, holly, maple, bell, and Buddhist gong (1271–75 respectively); battle helmets (1276–80); and Noh masks (1281–83).

1284-1300. Dragon (*ryu*). According to Japanese reference sources, the uninitiated can recognize a dragon by the following characteristics: 9,981 scales on its back; four legs and five claws per foot; horns like a deer; eyes like a demon; ears like a cow; beard; protruding jaw; and ferocious expression. It is variously reported as residing either in water or clouds, but in either case it

1251 1252 1253 1254 1255

1256 1257 1258 1259 1260

1261 1262 1263 1264 1265

1266 1267 1268 1269 1270

1271 1272 1273 1274 1275

is capable of leaping through the heavens, where it controls the thunder and summons the rain. The dragon is one of the most ancient of all images in China, and is traditionally associated with the unicorn, phoenix, and tortoise as one of the four auspicious creatures. Both its imperial and Buddhist associations were transferred to Japan, and it was particularly associated with Zen. In a legend possibly based on the discovery of iron in Japan, the *Kojiki* recounts how the god Susano-o slew an eight-headed dragon and found a sword embedded in its tail (cf. 1289). As a design, the dragon can be represented by its tail (1289–90), claws (1291–93), and scales (1294–95). A variant representation, the *amaryu,* or "rain dragon," was also used in Japanese heraldry (1296–1300).

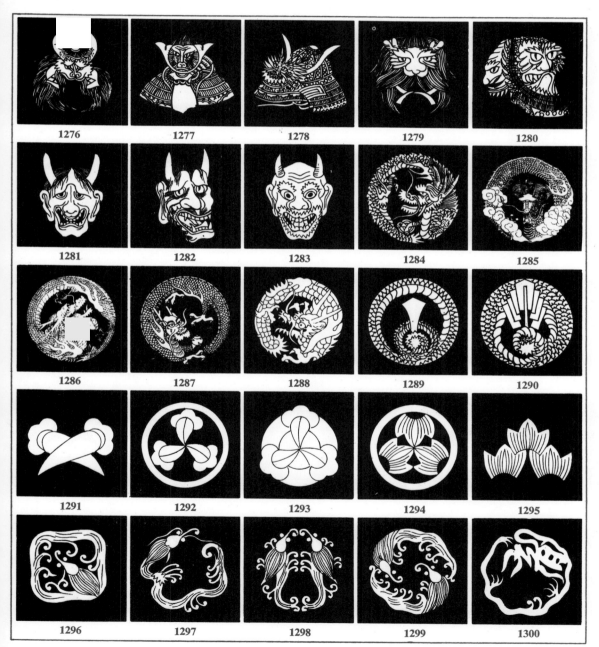

1276	1277	1278	1279	1280
1281	1282	1283	1284	1285
1286	1287	1288	1289	1290
1291	1292	1293	1294	1295
1296	1297	1298	1299	1300

1301-2. Dragonfly (*tombo*). During the period of feudal warfare, the dragonfly is reputed to have been an especially popular design applied to arrow quivers, and some warriors adopted it as a family crest. One reason for this was the insect's alternative names of *katsu mushi* and *shogun mushi,* both meaning "victory insect."

1303-5. Falcon (*taka*). Despite Buddhist injunctions against the taking of life, and thus against hunting (not to mention war), falconry was a highly esteemed sport not only among the warrior class, but among some of the emperors themselves.

Even in the Heian period, the court bureaucracy included an Office of Falconry. The warriors, of course, admired the bird for its fierce, combative spirit, but since it was difficult to draw, only a few actually adopted it as a battlefield emblem. Instead, many used the falcon feather as a mark.

1306-25. Feather (*takanoha*). The feather motif in Japanese heraldry invariably represents the feather of a falcon, and thus the martial connotations mentioned above are implicit. The association was enhanced by the resemblance of this design to the feathers on an arrow (*see* 1494–1535).

In addition, during the feudal period it was customary for military officers to display falcon feathers at the side of their headgear. Several shrines, such as those of Higo and Aso, adopted the falcon feather as their official emblem, thus providing a religious dimension stressed by many families who later used this as a family crest.

1326-50. Goose (*kari*). In the Heian period, a distant flight of wild geese was depicted by the simple and familiar convention of a single V-shaped stroke to represent the wings of each bird. When this convention was adapted to heraldic design, a

bird's head was introduced into the "V," thus creating the rather idiosyncratic style depicted below (1334–41). A variant of this variant produced the "knotted goose" (1342–50). As a formal heraldic device, these two styles were far more popular than more realistic depictions such as 1326–33.

1326 1327 1328 1329 1330

1331 1332 1333 1334 1335

1336 1337 1338 1339 1340

1341 1342 1343 1344 1345

1346 1347 1348 1349 1350

1351-52. Heron (*sagi*). This is an incidental motif, and not a formal category in Japanese heraldry. Crest 1352 below is a variation on the paulownia leaf, and is generally presented under that heading.

1353-55. Horse (*uma*). As revealed by the clay *haniwa* figurines of the prehistoric period, the horse and mounted warrior have long been a major element in Japanese society. Even during the peaceful centuries of the Heian period, horseracing was a popular pastime, and in the feudal period the warrior-aristocrat was distinguished by the fact that he could afford to ride to battle. Despite

these clearly martial associations, the horse was a rare motif among family crests—undoubtedly because it was difficult to draw. Equestrian gear, on the other hand, provided a popular motif in the form of the bit (*see* 1576–90) and tassel (*see* 2081–90).

1356-58. Lion (*shishi*). In both design and statuary, the lion had strong continental associations in early Japan. The particular rendering depicted below is believed to have originated in Persia and been transmitted to Japan only after passing through India, China, and Korea. The lion-and-peony pattern (1356–57), which has Buddhist associations,

was popular in the early Heian period, and from the Kamakura period this became an especially popular design on armor—elegant, religous, and fierce.

1359-62. Monkey (*saru*). Although the highly abstract "monkey" pattern (1359–61) appears in a number of Japanese books of crests, it does not appear to have been used as a formal family crest.

1363-65. Nightingale (*uguisu*). This, like the swallow, is a motif familiar to Japanese literature and art, but never a part of formal heraldry. In the Japanese world of gentle associations, the nightingale

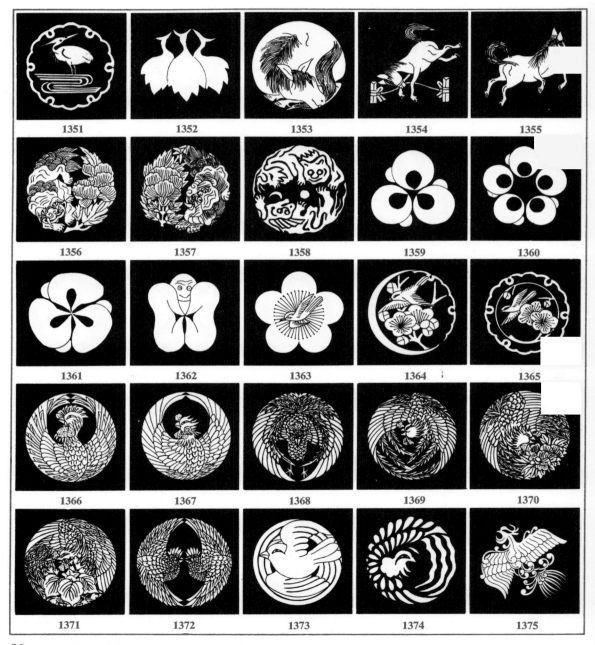

1351   1352   1353   1354   1355
1356   1357   1358   1359   1360
1361   1362   1363   1364   1365
1366   1367   1368   1369   1370
1371   1372   1373   1374   1375

belongs with the plum blossom just as the sparrow belongs with bamboo and the pigeon with mistletoe. Below it is depicted in a single blossom of the plum, with plum blossoms in a moon-and-cloud enclosure, and with blossoms in a "snow ring."

1366-75. Phoenix (*hoo*). Fortunately for art, depiction of the mythical phoenix did not maintain fidelity to its legendary description: front of the body like a goose; rear like a unicorn; head like a snake; tail like a fish, or alternatively a dragon; back like a tortoise; neck like a swallow; and beak like a chicken. The phoenix allegedly was seen only when a virtuous ruler appeared; that is, almost never.

1376-85. Pigeon (*hato*). Gentle envoy of the ungentle bodhisattva Hachiman, patron god of war, the pigeon was an auspicious sign of martial victory. The association may well have developed from the simple fact that flocks of pigeons are invariably found in the compounds of temples and shrines.

1386-88. Plover (*chidori*). The plover was first used as a pattern around the late Heian period. In the last design it carries a love letter.

1389-90. Quail (*uzura*). Like the heron, this is an incidental motif. The quail is shown among ears of millet.

1391-99. Rabbit (*usagi*). The white rabbit has numerous auspicious and quasi-religious associations in Japanese tradition. It was regarded as embodying the spirit of the moon; it appears in the myth cycle related in the *Nihon Shoki;* and it was associated in some early texts (e.g., the Heian-period *Engishiki*) with the tortoise and crane as a symbol of longevity.

1400. Rooster (*onagadori*). The crest actually depicts the *onagadori,* or longtailed cock, a real Japanese species with a tail that trails behind it to a distance of ten feet or more.

1376 — 1377 — 1378 — 1379 — 1380
1381 — 1382 — 1383 — 1384 — 1385
1386 — 1387 — 1388 — 1389 — 1390
1391 — 1392 — 1393 — 1394 — 1395
1396 — 1397 — 1398 — 1399 — 1400

1401-2. Sea Gull (*kamome*). Surprisingly for an island country, the sea gull does not appear as a motif in Japan's formal heraldry. The designs below are generally categorized under sails.

1403-25. Shell. Several varieties of sea shells appear as motifs in Japanese heraldry, among them the clam (*hamaguri*, 1403–11), sea fan (*itayagai*, 1412–22), helmet shell (*kabutogai*, 1423), roll shell (*kai*, 1424), and conch (*horagai*, 1425). In the Heian period, the clam shell played a small role in helping women and children in the courtly society to while away the time. A pastime known as "shell games" (*kaiawase*) involved competing to see who could most quickly match marked shells separated into two piles. The practice of writing poems and painting pictures on shells developed out of the *kaiawase*. In later years, shells painted gold and silver and marked with crests were scattered among the wedding gifts on the occasion of a marriage bringing together members of the court (*kuge*) and warrior (*buke*) elites. The shell of the edible sea fan was often used as a ladle or tureen, and appears to have been adopted for its decorative appearance. One family, the Igai, used this as a crest for denotative reasons. The conch was used as a horn both on the battlefield and in esoteric Buddhism, as well as by mountain ascetics, where it was ascribed magical qualities in dispelling sins, demons, and enemies.

1426-30. Shrimp (*ebi*). To celebrate the New Year, Japanese place bamboo, pine, and a large boiled shrimp over the door or gateway to their home. The auspicious connotations of the shrimp date from ancient times and are ascribed to a rather charming origin: due to its resemblance to a hunched-over old man, bearded and dignified, it is said, the shrimp bespeaks longevity. The Emi

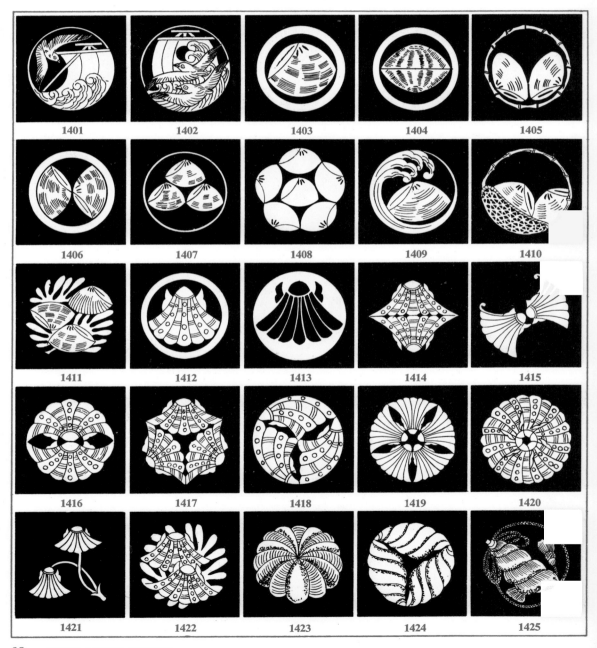

1401   1402   1403   1404   1405

1406   1407   1408   1409   1410

1411   1412   1413   1414   1415

1416   1417   1418   1419   1420

1421   1422   1423   1424   1425

family used this motif to convey a kind of counterpoint phonetic denotation.

1431-60. Sparrow (*suzume*). As revealed in a famous Japanese folk tale called *The Sparrow with the Cut Tongue* (*Shita-kiri Suzume*), the sparrow exemplifies the virtue of repaying one's obligations—and greater virtues than this were few indeed in traditional Japan. Like the lion and peony or the pigeon and mistletoe, the sparrow is commonly depicted with bamboo. The association is a natural one, since flocks of sparrows commonly alight in the bamboo groves, and in all likelihood

the sparrow as a motif by itself derived from the combined sparrow-and-bamboo design. Warriors in particular favored crests depicting two sparrows facing each other—a martial symbol of "confrontation."

The last two crests (1459–60) actually depict a different variety, the *bundori* (Java sparrow or "paddy bird").

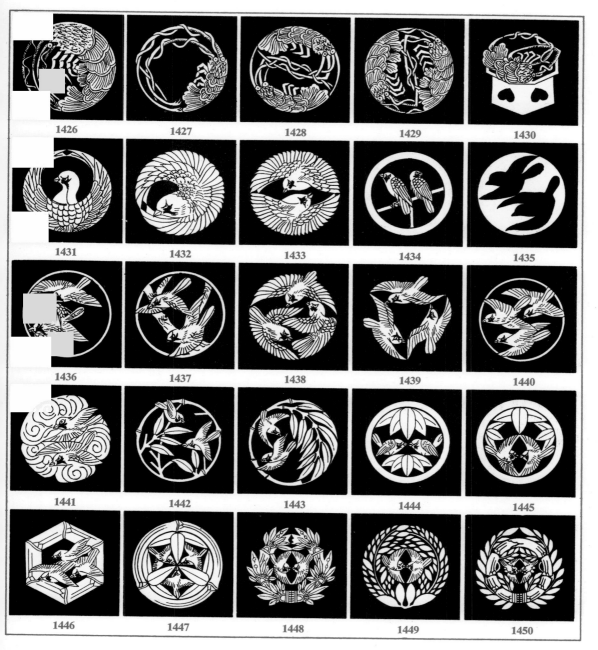

1461-65. Swallow (*tsubame*). This motif, like that of the nightingale, was never developed as a formal category in Japanese heraldic design. The swallow is depicted with water plantain, wisteria, and iris respectively in the first three crests.

1466-75. Tortoise (*kame*). In Chinese and Japanese legend, the crane was associated with one thousand years of life and the tortoise with ten thousand. Appropriately, Heian women frequently had these auspicious emblems engraved on the backs of their mirrors. The tortoise crest actually appears to be based upon a fresh-water turtle, and the long "tail" shown in many versions represents water grasses which have attached themselves to the shell. These enhance the impression of age and give the tortoise an alternative name, *minokame* or "straw-raincoat turtle." In Shinto, the tortoise was also associated with the shrines of Matsuo and Izumo.

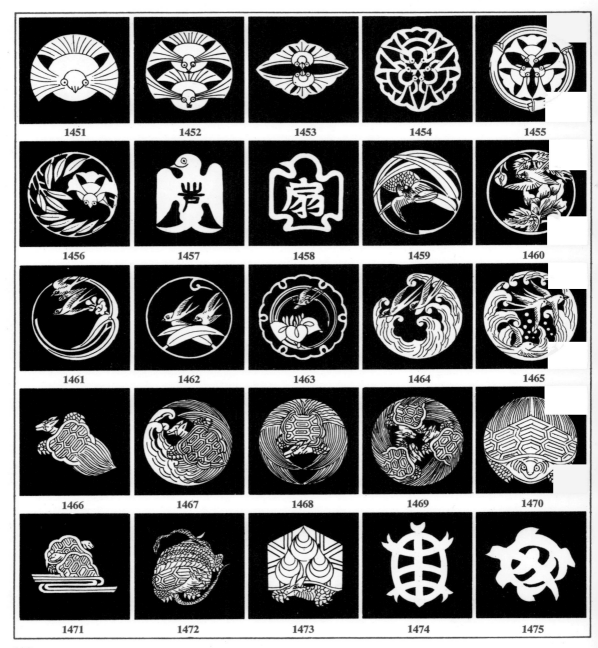

1451	1452	1453	1454	1455
1456	1457	1458	1459	1460
1461	1462	1463	1464	1465
1466	1467	1468	1469	1470
1471	1472	1473	1474	1475

Man-made Objects

1476-93. Amulet (*Gion mamori*). As its Japanese name makes clear, this amulet or talisman was associated primarily with Kyoto's Yasaka Shrine, more familiarly known as the Gion Shrine. The shrine was said to be associated with the legendary emperor Gozu, whose name is written with two ideographs meaning literally "cow's head," and some scholars hold that originally the amulet was designed to resemble a cow's head. Another association of the shrine was with Yakushi, god of healing.

Originally the Gion amulet seems to have been used as a crest by per- sons who worshiped at this particular shrine. It achieved its greatest re- nown in the Edo period, however, when "hidden Christians" such as the Ikeda family of Bizen adopted the amulet as a family crest after Chris- tianity had been proscribed in Japan. Their selection was based on the "hidden cross" contained in this traditional design.

1494-1535. Archery Items. In tradi- tional Japanese literature, the way of the warrior was sometimes described as "the way of the bow and arrow" (*bushi no yumiya no michi*), and this readily lent itself to one of the more obviously martial motifs in Japanese heraldry. Various elements were singled out and emphasized. Because they were easy to draw and readily identifiable, the most popular archery crests highlighted either the arrow notch (*yahazu*, 1494–1502) or arrow feathers (*yabane*, 1503–18). Crests depicting the entire arrow (*ya*, 1519– 27) are rarer. Three types of ar- rowhead used by Japanese warriors appear in the arrow designs: the ordinary pointed tip (*heigen*, 1519), "frog's legs" (*karimata*, 1522), and "humming bulb" (*narikabura*, 1527). The last gave off a whirring sound, and was used to initiate battles. The arrowhead alone (*yajiri*, 1528) was

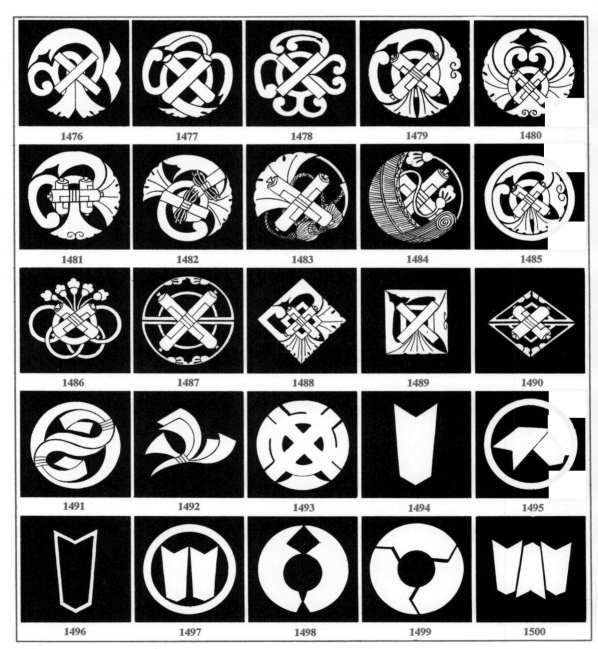

1476 1477 1478 1479 1480
1481 1482 1483 1484 1485
1486 1487 1488 1489 1490
1491 1492 1493 1494 1495
1496 1497 1498 1499 1500

rarely used as a motif, and bows (*yumi*, 1529–30) were also not a popular design—probably because they did not lend themselves to bold graphic treatment. Even prior to the period of feudal strife, archery was a popular pastime among the upper classes, but despite this fact the use of targets (*mato*, 1531–35) as a motif for formal crests did not appear until the Edo period, when some shopkeepers adopted this as an emblem.

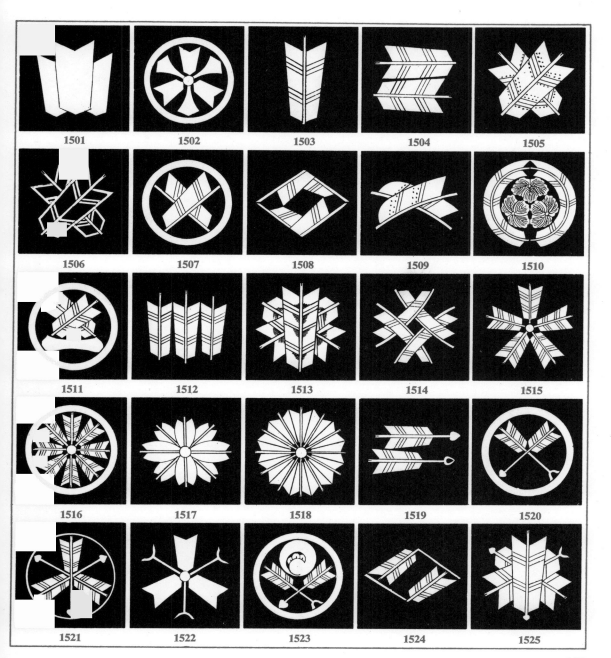

1501   1502   1503   1504   1505

1506   1507   1508   1509   1510

1511   1512   1513   1514   1515

1516   1517   1518   1519   1520

1521   1522   1523   1524   1525

1536-42. Axe (*masakari*). The *masakari* is a large battle-axe originally used in ancient China. Although passing reference to it appears in some Japanese war chronicles (such as the *Taiheiki*), it was never an important part of Japanese warfare. It is thus interesting that, when receiving investiture in office from the emperor, a new shogun was presented with this atypical weapon.

The axe also had superstitious and auspicious connotations. Among mountain ascetics, who probably originally used it to clear away the brush, it became a symbolic implement for driving off evil spirits.

Also, by one of the inimitable Japanese puns, the *ono* or small axe can also be read *yoki*—and *yoki* in turn can mean "good."

1543-45. Ball (*mari*). Among the traditional upper classes, men amused themselves with a "kickball" (*shumari*, 1543) made usually of deerskin, while women and children devised games with lovely balls made of colored silk threads (*kinumari*, 1544–45). Neither motif was part of formal heraldry.

1546-60. Battledore and Shuttlecock (*hagoita to hane*). This game, now generally associated with New Year's festivities in Japan, became

fashionable among upper class women and children around the Muromachi period. Despite prohibitive sumptuary legislation, elaborately painted battledores, some even wound with gold and silver thread, became one of the famous products of Edo during the Edo period. Neither the battledore (*hagoita*, 1546–54) nor shuttlecock (*hane*, 1552–60) motifs ever entered the mainstream of Japanese heraldry, although both are commonly included in traditional books of crests.

1561-75. Bell (*suzu; hansho*). Primarily associated with dances performed in Shinto shrines, the delicate

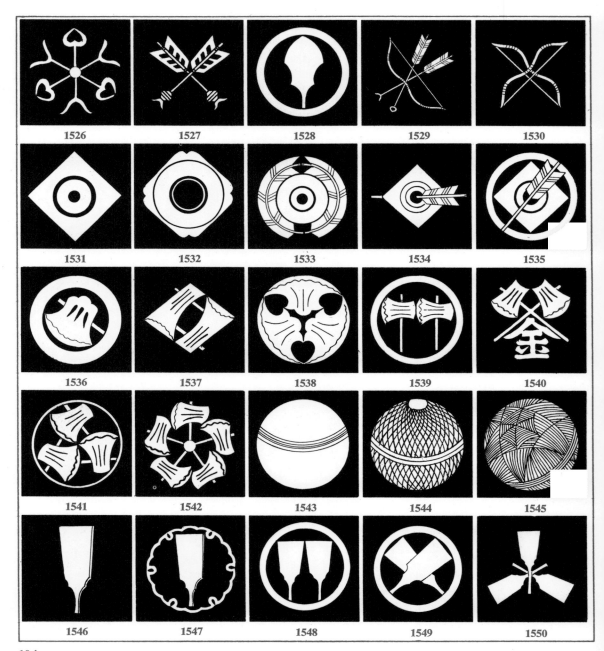

suzu (1561–68) in time came to be used by the Japanese both as a purely musical instrument and as an accessory which was sometimes worn on festive occasions, attached to items such as mirrors, bows, and swords, or affixed to such animals as horses and falcons. The second type of bell depicted below is the *hansho,* or fire bell (1569–75), which was rung by being struck from the outside (*see* 1573). During the Edo period, warriors deprived of war found a martial surrogate in fire brigades and fire-fighting.

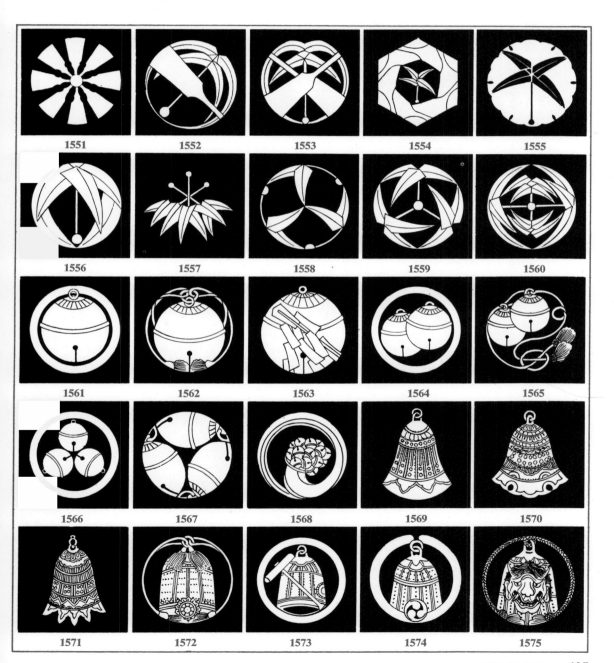

1551	1552	1553	1554	1555
1556	1557	1558	1559	1560
1561	1562	1563	1564	1565
1566	1567	1568	1569	1570
1571	1572	1573	1574	1575

1576-90. Bit (*kutsuwa*). These small pieces on each side of the horse's bit not only gave a martial impression when used as crest motifs, but also were later adopted by several Christian families because of the "hidden cross" design.

1591-92. Bowl and Chopsticks (*gosu ni hashi*). The circle representing a certain type of lacquered bowl (*gosu*), together with parallel lines representing chopsticks, appears to be a mark first used as a seal in ancient times. It was reputedly adopted by the founder of the Narita family to commemorate an occasion when having run out of provisions and

faced with an imminent battle, he entered a mountain shrine, ate the offering of rice placed there, and, thus fortified, acquitted himself in the day's business with distinction.

1593-1610. Bridge of a Musical Instrument (*kotoji; koma*). The bridge under each string of the thirteen-stringed *koto* (*kotoji*, 1593–1600) was first adopted as a design during the Kamakura period and later used as a family crest by several families. Three plectrums enclosed by *koto* bridges are shown in 1600. In the Edo period, the three-stringed samisen became a favorite instrument in the pleasure quarters, and its bridge

(*koma,* 1601–10) was introduced as a design at this late date.

1611-12. Brush (*fude*). Calligraphy is one of the major arts in the Orient, and until recent times all handwriting was done with a brush such as those depicted here.

1613-15. Buddhist Utensils (*katsuma; shakujo*). The *katsuma* (1613–14), which appears to have been originally a harpoon-like weapon in ancient India, was used in esoteric Buddhism to drive out evil passions. The crests represent two of these instruments crossed. The *shakujo* (1615) was originally a staff carried by monks and ascetics, and later was

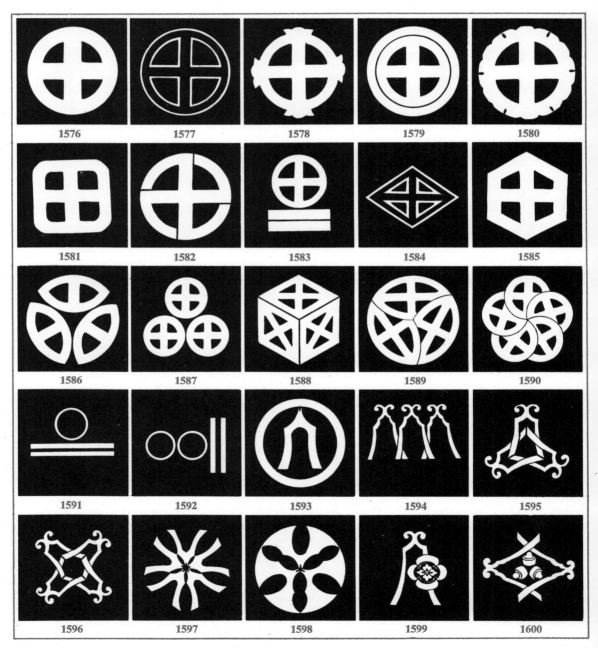

ascribed magical qualities for driving off poisonous snakes and even demons. Only the top of the staff is depicted in the crest.

1616-20. Candle (*rosoku*). The candle emblem first appeared in the Edo period, when it was used as a shop sign by makers of candles.

1621-25. Chess Piece (*koma*). *Shogi*, the chess played in the Orient, was transmitted to Japan from China during the T'ang dynasty. Each person controls twenty men on a board with eighty-one squares. The game became especially popular in the Muromachi period.

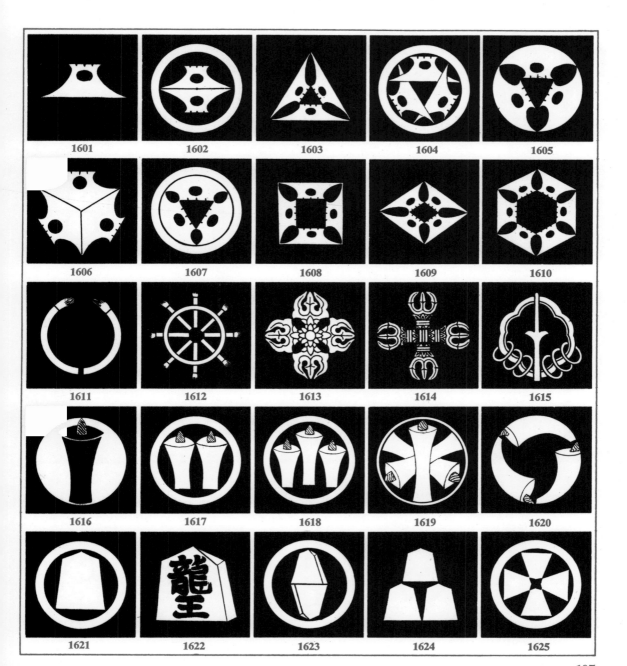

1601	1602	1603	1604	1605
1606	1607	1608	1609	1610
1611	1612	1613	1614	1615
1616	1617	1618	1619	1620
1621	1622	1623	1624	1625

1626-37. Coin (*sen*). In a society said to despise both merchants and money, the appearance of coins as a heraldic motif may seem surprising. During the heart of the feudal period, Japan did not mint her own coins but instead imported copper currency from Ming China; from the twelfth century, in fact, this was one of Japan's principal imports from China. The *Eiraku tsuho* (1626, 31 below) was the most familiar of the imported coins, widely circulated throughout the Muromachi and Edo periods; yearly rice tribute was reckoned on the basis of this coin. From the year 1636, during the Kan'ei era, Japan resumed minting after a lapse of several centuries and produced the *Kan'ei tsuho;* although the Kan'ei era lasted only from 1624 to 1643, subsequent mintings continued to bear this marking (1627 below). Both Eiraku and Kan'ei, while signifying chronological periods, are auspicious words, meaning "eternal happiness" and "generous eternity." Coins used as a crest also reflected the Buddhist practice of placing six coins alongside a dead person so that he might navigate the six paths of the afterworld, paying alms to the six *jizo,* or gods, along the way. It meant, in short, safe passage.

1638-39. Comb (*akadori*). Literally "red bird," the shape of the comb derives from an idiosyncratic pun on "dandruff remover" (*akadori*), and its introduction as a crest was understandably not greatly emulated.

1640. Cord (*agemaki*). This decorative cord, used on both furnishings and armor, was adopted as a crest by several families in the Muromachi period.

1641-50. Cotton (*yuiwata*). Bound bundles of cotton—the only form depicted in Japanese design—were used as religious offerings and as felicitous gifts at marriage ceremonies.

1651-70. Decoration (*noshi*). Originally made of strips of dried abalone, the graceful *noshi* decoration is still applied to gifts in Japan, though usually made of folded paper. It carries a happy import similar to the bound cotton—possibly based on a pun on *noshi* as meaning "to expand or extend"; that is, to prosper.

1671-5. Doll (*mamezo*). Literally, "made of beans," the *mamezo* was a balancing doll which became popular in the Edo period. Its name derived from the generic label applied to street entertainers, whose label in turn derived from the personal name of a street acrobat named Mame-

zo (literally, "bean storehouse") who enjoyed considerable fame in the Genroku era.

1651	1652	1653	1654	1655
1656	1657	1658	1659	1660
1661	1662	1663	1664	1665
1666	1667	1668	1669	1670
1671	1672	1673	1674	1675

1676-90. Drum (*tsuzumi*). Not introduced as a design motif until late in the feudal period, the small hand drum actually had a long history in Japan, dating back to the Sarugaku mimetic dances of the Heian period. It later became a basic ingredient in Japanese folk music, narrative songs, Noh, and Kabuki.

1691-92. Dumpling (*dango*). The dumpling as a crest has an unappetizing origin in the avowed comment of Oda Nobunaga, Japan's great sixteenth-century unifier, that he wished to see the severed heads of his enemies skewered like dumplings on a spit.

1693-1750. Fan (*ogi; sensu; uchiwa*). The folding fan (*ogi* or *sensu*, 1693–1720) originated in Japan and became so prized by the Chinese that by the twelfth century it was one of the major Japanese export items to the continent. Usually made of bamboo and paper, it was admired not only for its beauty and practical use in a very humid climate, but also for its "auspicious" qualities. The opening and broadening of the fan was cited as symbolic of the development of things, and one of the alternative words for fan, *suehiro,* literally means "end wide." As a design motif, the fan was widely admired in the Heian and Kamakura periods in particular.

The cypress fan (*hiogi,* 1721–25) was used as a formal part of traditional court costume, with the number of slats varying according to age, sex, and rank—the higher the status, the fewer the slats.

Unlike the folding fan, the round fan (*uchiwa,* 1726–31) and military fan (*gumbai uchiwa,* 1732–45) were of Chinese origin, and both had military significance. The round fan, which was sometimes very large, occasionally was placed at the tip of various heraldic devices such as the *sashimono* and *umajirushi.* In the Edo

period, the likenesses of popular actors were printed on round fans and sold to urbanites.

The "military fan" received its name belatedly, for it was originally known to Heian court circles simply as "China [or T'ang] round fan" (*kara uchiwa*). Made of metal, leather, or bamboo, it was usually lacquered and elaborately decorated. Its martial nomenclature developed in the feudal period when high officers used the fan to direct their troops in battle, much as Western officers might use a sword or baton. In time, the military fan took on a religious dimension, as it came to be

regarded as one of the special possessions of Marishiten, a god of war. Furthermore, as sumo wrestling became a national sport, the military fan took on yet another role, being held by the referee and used to point out the winner in each match. Thus the fan also became highly auspicious.

The feather fan (*hauchiwa*, 1746–50) as a motif actually derives from the hemp palm design (*see* 636–45), and in some cases is virtually identical with its parent design. Identified as a fan, however, it is immediately associated with the *tengu,* or supernatural beings who peopled desolate

places. Probably through this association, the feather fan was adopted as a symbol by certain temples and shrines associated with mountain asceticism, and as a family crest it thus had clear religious connotations.

A famous commemorative fan crest is the fan-with-the-rising-sun of the Nasu family, which derived from a celebrated incident during the closing stages of the Gempei War. The Taira forces had fled by ship to the Inland Sea, where the Minamoto caught up with them and confronted them from the shore near Yashima. Dusk was falling, and both sides were preparing to retire for the night when

1701 1702 1703 1704 1705

1706 1707 1708 1709 1710

1711 1712 1713 1714 1715

1716 1717 1718 1719 1720

1721 1722 1723 1724 1725

a small boat separated itself from the Taira fleet and drew within approximately ninety yards of the shoreline. In a gesture reflecting the courtly grace which survived even that bitter war, a young woman in the boat hung a red fan with a circular rising sun on it to a pole on the gunwale, obviously daring the Minamoto to strike it down. The task fell to one Yoichi Munetaka, a twenty-year-old son of the Nasu family and the most skillful archer among the Minamoto forces. Yoichi, riding his horse into the shallows and praying fervently to the war god Hachiman and to the deities of his native place, loosed an arrow that struck the fluttering fan above the rivet and sent it spinning into the breeze. His descendants, with good reason, subsequently adopted as their family crest the design of a fan with a circular sun on it.

1751-56. Feather Duster (*haboki*). A puzzling emblem for a class which did not do its own dusting, as a heraldic device this may reflect devotion to the tea ceremony, where the feather brush had a firm ritualistic place.

1757-60. Fence (*mizugaki*). The highly formal Japanese name of this crest indicates that it specifically represents the fence which surrounds the compound of a Shinto shrine, and it is accordingly an explicitly religious motif.

1761-65. Flag (*hinomaru*). A popular pattern from the late Heian period, the plain *hinomaru* circle actually means "sun disc." It was adopted as an official national emblem only after the Japanese beheld the flags displayed by Commodore Perry in 1854. That same year, the Japanese Navy adopted the circular sun as their emblem, and this became the national flag in 1870.

1766-72. Gong (*choban*). Once used as a musical instrument in China, the gong was most conspicu-

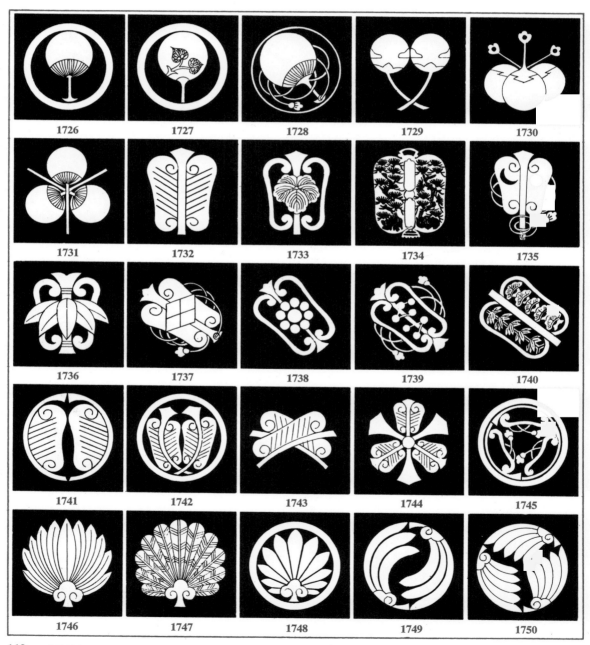

ously used in Zen temples in Japan to summon monks to services, meditation, meals, and the like. As a crest it generally signified that its bearer was a believer in Zen, although the graceful shape of the instrument also led to its popular adoption.

1773-75. Hairpin (*kogai*). An ornamental bodkin originally made of luxurious material such as silver, gold, ivory, tortoise shell, quartz, or agate, this was first used by the rich, but gradually became fashionable among women of all classes. As a design it appeared late in the feudal period, and played no role in formal heraldry.

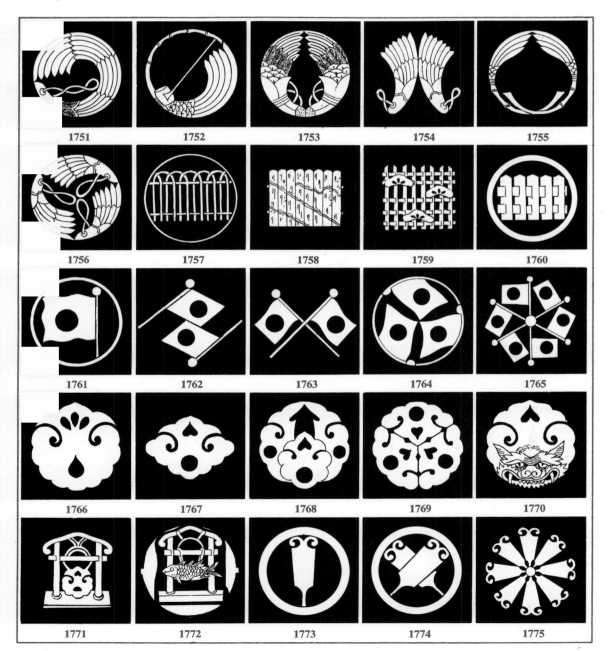

1776-95. Handle (*kan*). Although probably a purely ornamental and nonrepresentational design in origin, over the centuries this motif acquired the label *kan*, denoting its resemblance to the metal handles traditionally used on chests of drawers. As such it is commonly classified under man-made objects. Very possibly the "handle" motif represents an early abstract version of the popular *mokko*, or "melon," pattern. It is used as an elegant and versatile enclosure in much the same manner.

1796-1839. Headgear (*kasa, zuhin; eboshi; kabuto*). The nomenclature of Japanese headgear is a haber-

dasher's delight, and many of the various labels appear also in the catalogue of Japanese crests. As patterns, the following general categories can be noted: sedge hats (*kasa*, 1796–1808); "umbrella hats" (*jingusa*, 1809; *kasa hoko*, 1810); military hats (*ashigarugasa*, 1811; *jingasa*, 1812–13; and *amigasa*, 1814–15); cowls (*zuhin*, 1816–19); formal and semiformal headgear (*eboshi*, 1820–25); and battle helmets (*kabuto*, 1826–39).

The sedge hat had patrician rather than peasant associations in traditional Japan, and thus it was not anomalous that the haughty upper

classes developed this as a design. From the middle of the Heian period, upper-class women and children commonly wore the *kasa* as protection against rain, snow, and sun. A high-peaked variation known as the *tokiwagasa* (1797, 1808) took its name from the mother of the famous Minamoto Yoshitsune, and a variation of this called the "hunting-preserve hat" (*karibagasa*, 1801) was worn on hunting excursions by warriors from the Kamakura period. The elaborate "umbrella hats" were worn on festive and religious occasions, and completely concealed the wearer's face; they could be either

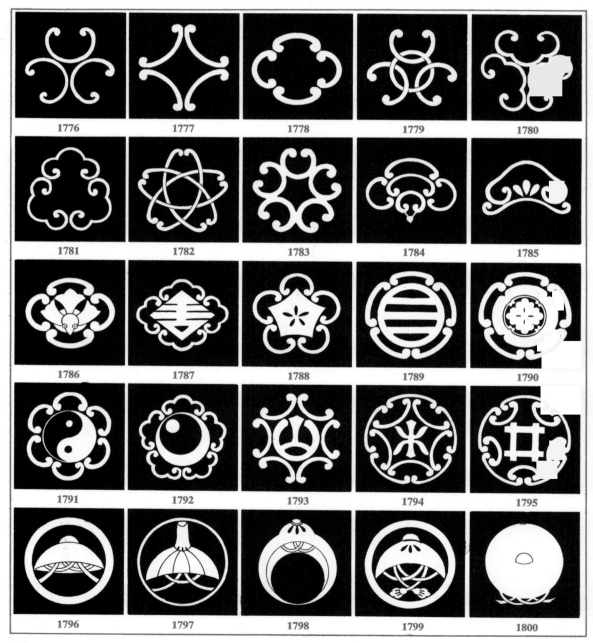

1776	1777	1778	1779	1780
1781	1782	1783	1784	1785
1786	1787	1788	1789	1790
1791	1792	1793	1794	1795
1796	1797	1798	1799	1800

worn or carried on poles, as shown below. By an auspicious pun, *kasa* could come to mean "increase" or "enlarge."

Military hats, made of metal or thickly woven rush, appeared comparatively late in the feudal period and were worn by low-ranking warriors and soldiers. The formal *eboshi* developed over the course of several centuries from the court headgear associated with the system of "cap ranks" which had been instituted in the early seventh century. Originally made of black silk and worn in a prescribed manner according to the individual's rank, by the middle of the feudal period it was being made of lacquered paper and had become popular headgear among the commoners.

The cowl was originally worn under court headgear, but was put to more practical purposes in the Edo period when lovers going to an assignation used it to conceal their identity. As such, it emerged belatedly as a design motif most closely associated with the tastes of the floating world of the pleasure quarters.

The complex Japanese battle helmet was used on the battlefield from the early Kamakura period through-out the ensuing several centuries of bloodletting, but, surprisingly, it did not appear as a crest until the late feudal period. As the depictions below reveal, the helmet was designed not merely to protect the wearer's head but his soul as well—many carry religious emblems—and simultaneously to unnerve his opponent by a menacing appearance (cf. 1271–83). In the mayhem of medieval battle, a distinctive helmet served the practical purpose of enabling its wearer to make his identity known.

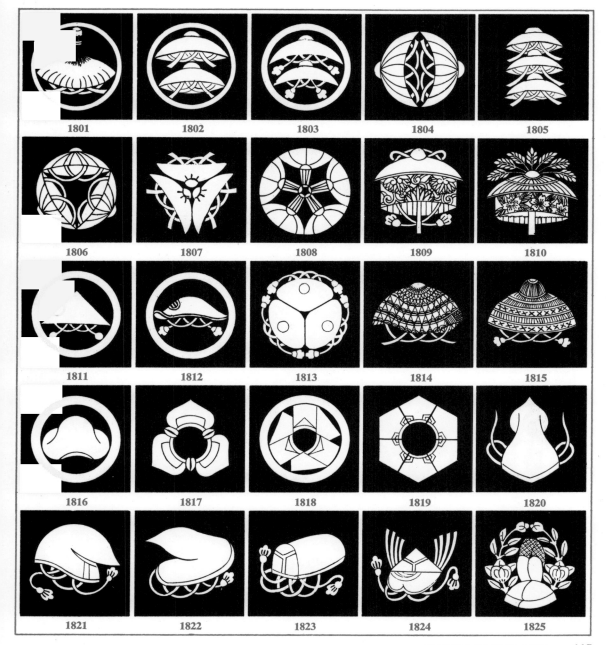

1801 1802 1803 1804 1805
1806 1807 1808 1809 1810
1811 1812 1813 1814 1815
1816 1817 1818 1819 1820
1821 1822 1823 1824 1825

1840-45. Helmet Crest (*kuwagata*). The ornamental "horns" found on many battle helmets derived their name from their resemblance to the blade of a hoe (*kuwa*).

1846-50. Hermitage (*iori*). The theme of withdrawal from worldly affairs pervades Japanese literature, but the stylized design of the hermitage seems to have made its appearance only in the Edo period, when it was adopted by several high-ranking warrior families as a family crest.

1851. Imperial Regalia (*sanshu shinki*). The sword, mirror, and *magatama* jewel have been imperial symbols since protohistoric times.

1852-57. Jewel (*hoju*). Associated with the dragon from ancient times, and therefore credited with vaguely auspicious connotations, the jewel—particularly with flames—was mainly associated with Buddhism by the Japanese. In esoteric teachings it was sometimes called the *niyoi hoju* and signaled the fulfillment of one's wishes.

1858-65. Kettle Rest (*kamashiki*). Like the handle crest, this may have derived from an earlier design, the *kanawa,* or interlocked rings pattern (*see* 2236–50), and assumed a label and identity of its own. It first appeared in the Edo period.

1866-71. Key (*kagi*). The traditional Japanese key (1866–69) may have been regarded as auspicious, since it was primarily associated with the storehouse, where a family's most treasured possessions were kept. The round key appeared under Western influence in the Meiji era and played no role in traditional design.

1872-76. Knot (*takaramusubi*). Literally "treasure knot," these elaborate decorations, still widely used today, developed within the popular culture of the late feudal period and were not a traditional design.

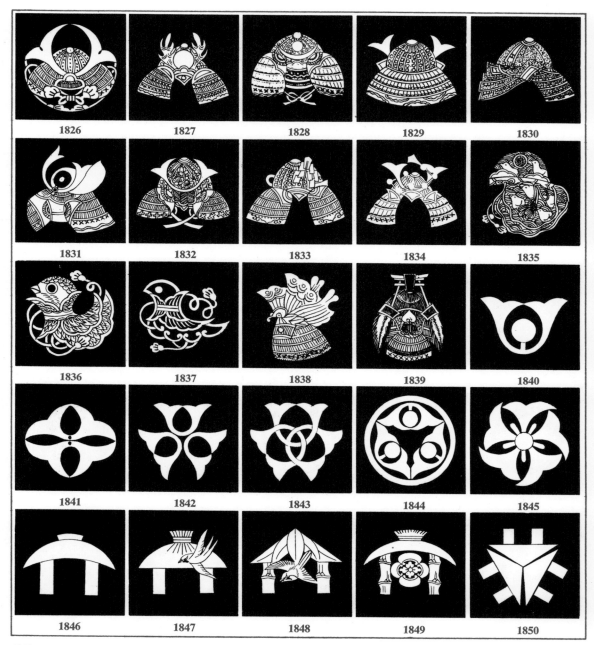

1851	1852	1853	1854	1855
1856	1857	1858	1859	1860
1861	1862	1863	1864	1865
1866	1867	1868	1869	1870
1871	1872	1873	1874	1875

1877-78. Ladder (*hashigo*). Several daimyo used this as an emblem, possibly with the implication of rising in the world.

1879-85. Letter (*fumi*). The "next morning letter" (*kinuginu no fumi*) exchanged between lovers is one of the most bittersweet devices of the classic *The Tale of Genji*. The practice continued into the Edo period, when love letters—folded and tied in a knot—appeared as a fitting design motif among denizens of the floating world.

1886-94. Mallet (*tsuchi*). The wooden mallet carried both martial and auspicious connotations. It sug-

gested striking and flattening out one's enemy, and at the same time was particularly associated with Daikoku, one of the Seven Gods of Good Fortune.

1895. Mask (*shishi kashira*). The Lion Dance and the mask used in it were brought to Japan from T'ang China and assimilated in a variety of Japanese dances, culminating in the *daikagura* (great kagura dances) of the Edo period.

1896-1915. Measure (*masu*). The size of bulk measures was standardized in Japan in 1669, and the measure motif appeared thereafter. It was particularly popular as a shop sign

among merchants, not only because of its appropriateness to their trade, but also because the word *masu* punned on a different ideograph meaning to increase or prosper. The most famous example of this crest was the three nesting measures (1913) used by the great line of Kabuki actors descending from Ichikawa Danjuro.

1916-17. Mirror (*kagami*). A surprisingly rare and incidental motif given its various associations with wealth, magic, and the sun, the mirror was always represented by one of the two stylized forms below (*see also* 1851; 2043).

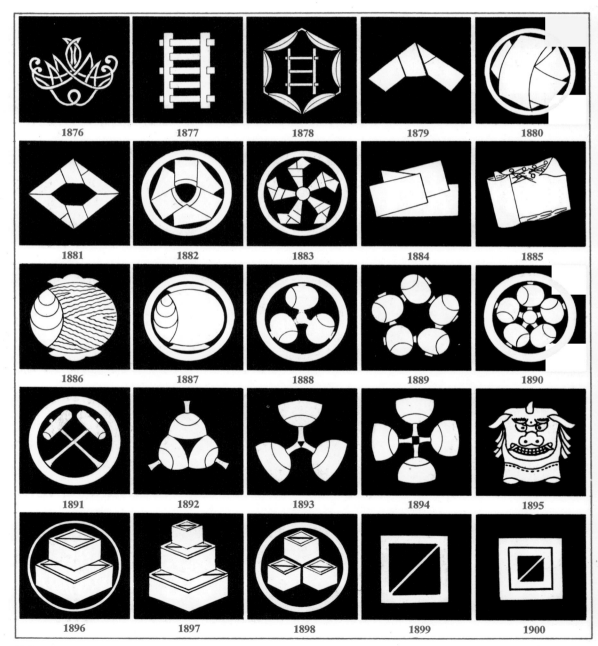

1876   1877   1878   1879   1880

1881   1882   1883   1884   1885

1886   1887   1888   1889   1890

1891   1892   1893   1894   1895

1896   1897   1898   1899   1900

118   MAN-MADE OBJECTS

1918-25. Net (*ami*). The fishing net, or mesh of the net, is one of the very few motifs—along with waves and crests dealing with sailing vessels and gear—that even suggests Japan's situation as a country surrounded by ocean. Its use as a crest motif appears to have been primarily auspicious, as reflected in the popular expression *ichimo dajin*, "a big haul with a single cast."

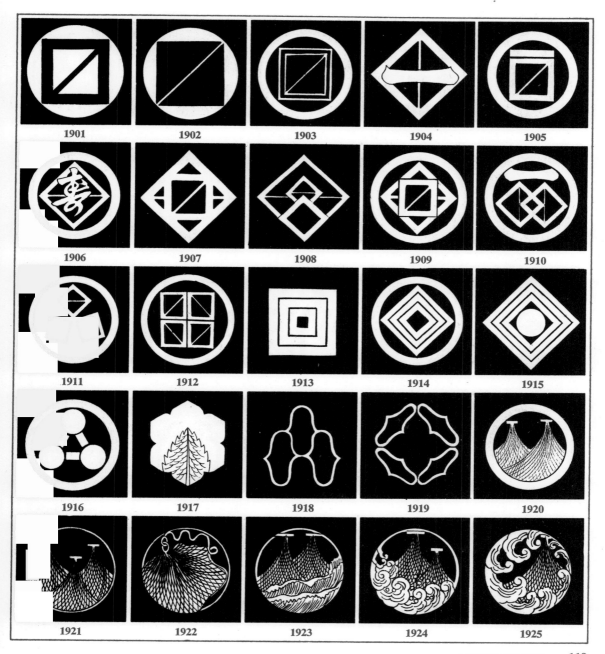

1901	1902	1903	1904	1905
1906	1907	1908	1909	1910
1911	1912	1913	1914	1915
1916	1917	1918	1919	1920
1921	1922	1923	1924	1925

1926-33. Pestle (*kine*). Primarily because of its use in making *mochi,* the sticky rice cake served on festive occasions, the pestle was regarded as a felicitous symbol in Japan. An ancient folk tale telling of the rabbit making *mochi* on the moon is represented in the last three crests below. The Komakine family, whose name literally meant "horse-tree-root," used the pestle crest as a pun on their own name.

1934-5. Plaque (*gaku*). The plaque is associated with shrines and temples in Japan, and the one with the ideographs for "twenty-eight" written on it (1934) alludes to the division of the celestial sphere into twenty-eight parts (*nijuhachi shuku*) in traditional geomancy. One family reputedly used a plaque crest because one of their members had presented for identification sixteen foes' heads on such objects.

1936-38. Pliers (*kuginuki*). Depiction of this tool, which was introduced into Japan only in recent times, probably stems from the established good associations accruing to the traditional "nail extractor" design (1937; *see* 2471–82).

1939-47. Pouches and Packages (*fukuro*). Small pouches or purses made of leather or embroidered material were worn at the waist, tucked into the sash of the kimono, and used to carry coins, amulets, personal seals, and the like. As a design motif, this bears a close resemblance to the depiction of the urn (2106–17). The squarer packages below (1946–47) are also identified as *fukuro* in Japanese, but look like the square wrapping cloths called *furoshiki.*

1948-50. Raft (*ikada*). A festive rather than practical conveyance, in early days when the court society flourished, rafts were festooned with flowers—especially cherry blossoms (1949)—and admired as they floated down a river or stream.

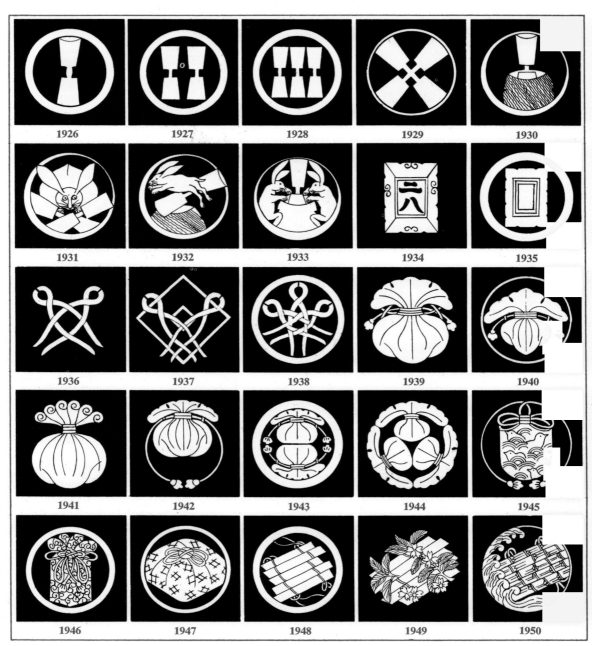

1951-2020. Sailing Vessels and Gear (*ho, hogakebune, kaji, kai, ikari*). Perhaps the most striking thing about maritime motifs in Japanese design is that they are exceedingly rare. Despite her geographic setting, Japan was not a seafaring nation during the period when heraldry flourished. Her artists, as the present collection reveals, turned their eyes overwhelmingly to the land and the products of the land. Motifs such as the wave or fisherman's net or sailing vessel represented little more than the view from the corner of the eye. They were few, and carried comparatively little prestige.

Unlike many other motifs, sailing vessels and sailing gear failed to collect an interesting lore or to develop levels of meaning. The Nawa of Kyushu reportedly used a sailing ship as their crest to commemorate their role in enabling the emperor Godaigo to escape his pursuers by fleeing the island by sea; crossed oars were used as a "hidden cross" by the Konishi family of Kyushu; the martial virtue of steadfastness was ascribed to the anchor; and that is about all. For the most part the crests below are what they appear to be: sail (*ho*, 1951–82); sailboat (*hogakebune*, 1983–92); rudder (*kaji*, 1993–96); oar (*kai*, 1997–

2005); and anchor (*ikari*, 2005–20). The traditional Japanese anchor was the claw, and the Western-style anchor (2019–20) appeared only in recent times.

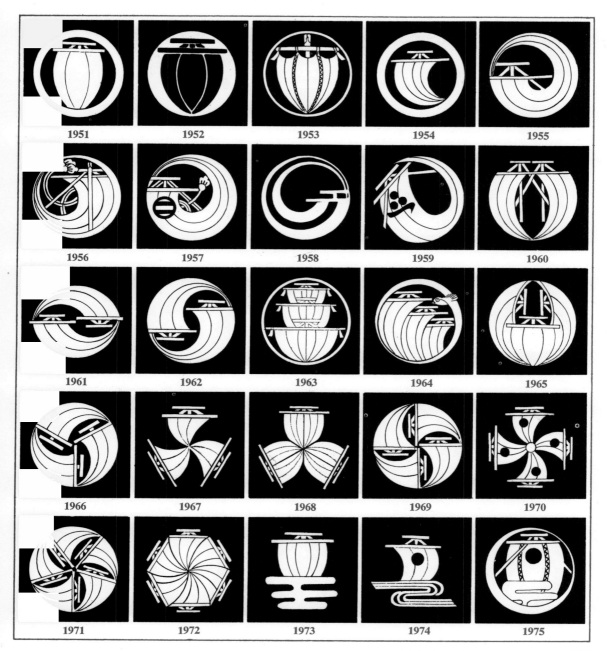

1951　1952　1953　1954　1955

1956　1957　1958　1959　1960

1961　1962　1963　1964　1965

1966　1967　1968　1969　1970

1971　1972　1973　1974　1975

2021-25. Scissors (*hasami*). Unlike Western shears, Japanese scissors are formed of a single piece of metal and manipulated by pinching the blade together. As a design motif, they first appeared in the seventeenth century.

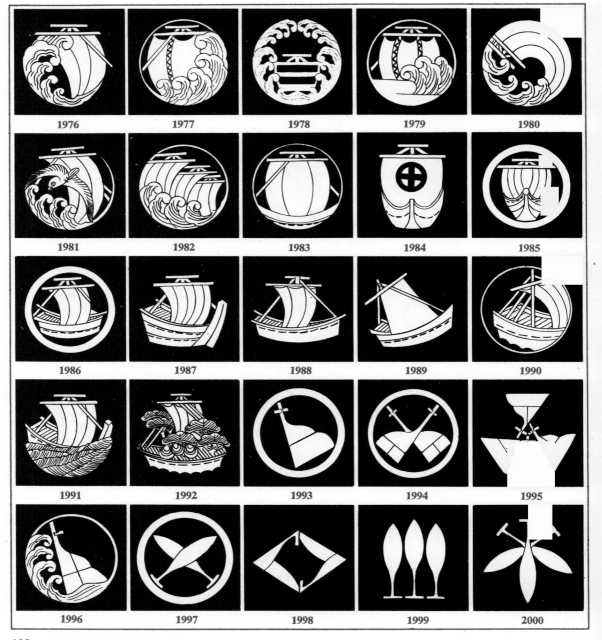

1976	1977	1978	1979	1980
1981	1982	1983	1984	1985
1986	1987	1988	1989	1990
1991	1992	1993	1994	1995
1996	1997	1998	1999	2000

2001   2002   2003   2004   2005

2006   2007   2008   2009   2010

2011   2012   2013   2014   2015

2016   2017   2018   2019   2020

2021   2022   2023   2024   2025

2026-32. Shinto Gateway (*torii*). In the myth cycle related in the earliest chronicles of Japan, it is recounted that when the Sun Goddess withdrew to a cavern, thus darkening the world, a cock sat outside crowing for her to come forth. According to some scholars, the distinctive Shinto gateway represents the perch on which the cock sat, while the straw rope often strung across the gateway was used to keep the goddess from reentering the cave once she had been enticed forth (*see* 2028-29). The ideographs with which *torii* is written literally mean "bird reside," which appears to lend etymological support to this theory. As a crest, the *torii* was used mostly by persons professionally associated with Shinto, but was also used denotatively by the Torii family.

2033-45. Shinto Pendant (*nusa; gohei*). The paper pendant intimately associated with Shinto worship underwent an interesting and profound development. In ancient times offerings of food, drink, and later cotton, hemp, and rough clothing were made to the deities. Eventually the latter offerings were replaced by symbolic strips of paper attached to a staff and called *gohei* or *nusa*, and in time the belief developed that these pendant papers, inevitably found on the Shinto altar, represented not offerings but the deities themselves. The token of worship had become the object of worship, and to the present day these strips are attached to straw ropes and signify the holiness of the place in which they are displayed.

The warrior class had deep faith in these. Men at war carried *gohei* aloft on their standards, affixed them to their helmets (*see* 1833), worked them into the design on their armor and quivers and the like, and wore them as family crests in a number of cases. Parishioners of the Kumano

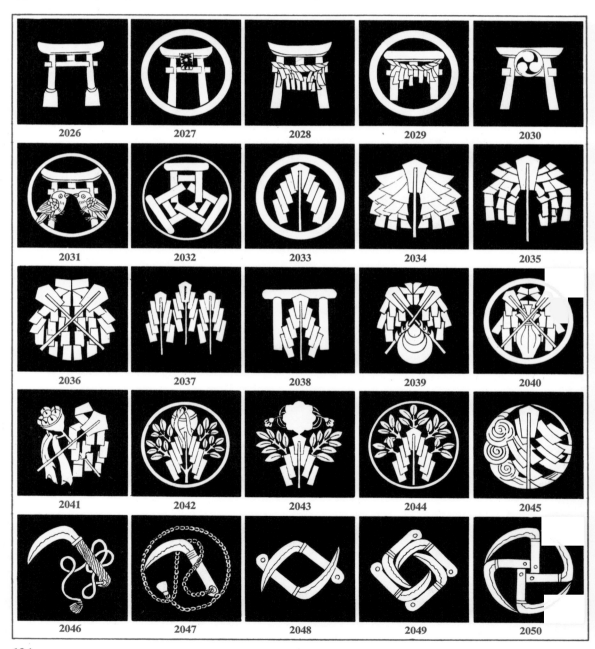

2026 · 2027 · 2028 · 2029 · 2030
2031 · 2032 · 2033 · 2034 · 2035
2036 · 2037 · 2038 · 2039 · 2040
2041 · 2042 · 2043 · 2044 · 2045
2046 · 2047 · 2048 · 2049 · 2050

Shrine may have used this as a crest to display their faith.

2046-50. Sickle (*kama*). The sickle was religious in import, being associated with the protective deity of the influential Suwa Shrine (*Suwa myojin*). It also signified cutting down one's enemies.

2051-75. Spools and Reels (*itomaki; chikiri*). Several versions of spools of thread (*itomaki*) appeared as design motifs in the late feudal period, among them reels of thread (2051–55), cards of thread (2055–58), and cards for thread (2059–62). These emblems may have been connected with the spinning trade.

A related but more puzzling design was the *chikiri*, ostensibly the warp wheel used in weaving (2062–75). Written with the same ideograph, *chikiri* also referred to a small joint used by architects and stone masons to connect wood or stone, and thus had the good connotation of reconciliation. It also punned on another word (*chigiri*) meaning to make a vow. Both of the latter associations appear to have lain behind adoption of the *chikiri* as a crest by several families.

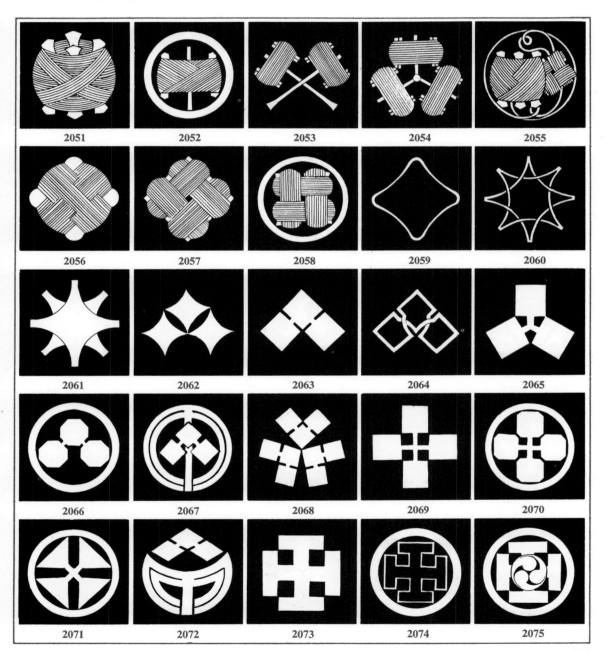

2076-80. Sword (*tsurugi*). In Japanese heraldry, the sword as a motif by itself was not only rare, but also failed to depict the actual sword used in battle by Japanese warriors. The latter was a gracefully curved and slender blade, which in quality rivaled even the Scythian sword. In crests, however, a broad, double-edged blade of Chinese origin was depicted—probably because it lent itself more readily to design. The latter style became a graphic convention introduced into literally hundreds of crests to give them a martial connotation for warrior families.

2081-90. Tassel (*gyoyo*). The puzzling "tassel" design, written with ideographs that literally mean "apricot leaf," appears to be a pattern which originated in Southwest Asia and eventually came to Japan through T'ang China. In both China and Japan, a tassel closely resembling the design was attached to the bridles and saddles of horses; in Japan it was also sometimes affixed to armor and carriages. The zingiber motif (*see* 1106–50) is based directly on this pattern, and frequently the two are virtually indistinguishable.

2091-95. Top (*koma*). The word for top is written with two ideographs meaning "independent pleasure," and from the Heian period this was indeed a popular source of enjoyment among Japanese children. The Japanese top, made of a single piece of wood, was stylized almost beyond recognition when it appeared as a crest motif in the late feudal period (2091–92). The top with a metal rod running through it represents Western versions of recent times.

2096-2100. Trivet (*gotoku*). The trivet was probably used as a motif because its name literally means the "five virtues" of Confucianism.

2101-5. Umbrella (*kasa*). Made of oiled paper and split bamboo, and

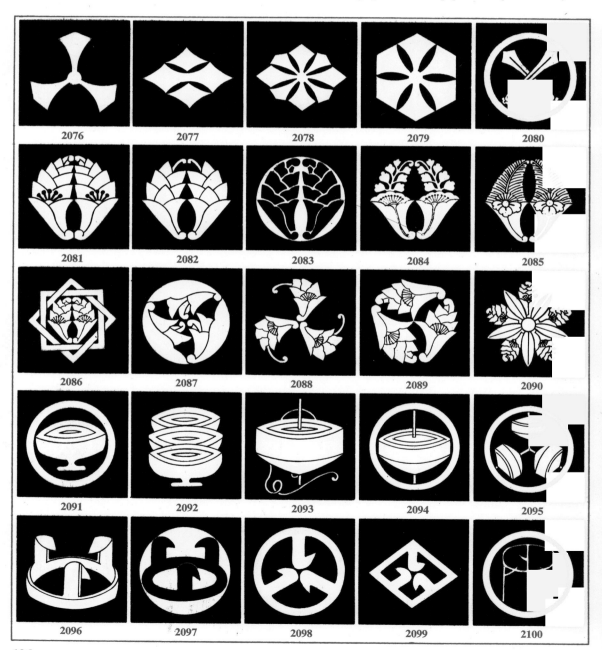

used against both rain and sun, the umbrella originally carried status connotations and was only gradually adopted for use by the commoners.

2106-17. Urn (*heishi*). A religious motif, the urn was used primarily to make offerings of saké to the Shinto deities.

2118-35. Weight (*fundo*). Made of copper and used on balance-type scales, the weight, like the measure, became especially popular as a shop sign in the Edo period. Several upper-class families, however, also used this as a family crest.

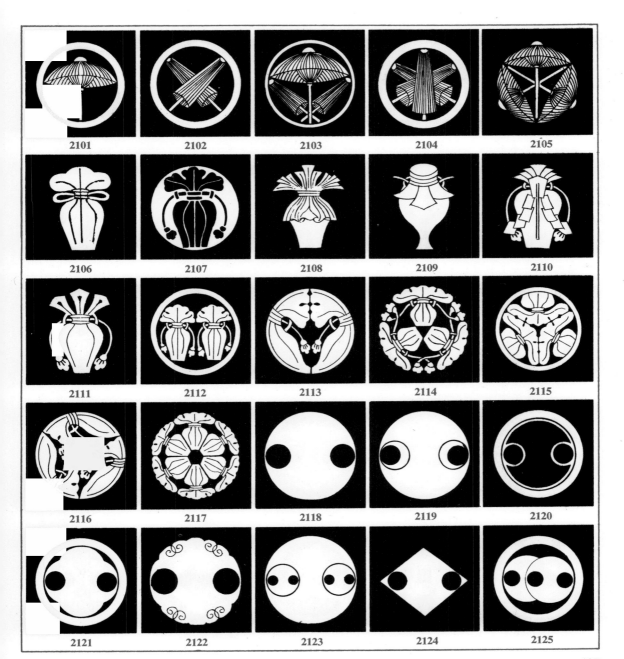

2136-75. Well Crib (*igeta; izutsu*). The well crib was one of the most popular motifs in Japanese heraldry and stands as an excellent example of the virtuosity of Japanese artists in elaborating upon a simple basic theme. Unlike many other motifs, it does not appear to have conveyed several layers of meaning, but was selected primarily for its simple beauty, and for denotative purposes. The latter function derived from the fact that a great variety of Japanese surnames contain the ideograph for *i,* or "well," in them—such as Inoue, Iguchi, Kawai, Imai, and the like. Other families used it as an enclosure.

2126	2127	2128	2129	2130
2131	2132	2133	2134	2135
2136	2137	2138	2139	2140
2141	2142	2143	2144	2145
2146	2147	2148	2149	2150

2151　　2152　　2153　　2154　　2155

2156　　2157　　2158　　2159　　2160

2161　　2162　　2163　　2164　　2165

2166　　2167　　2168　　2169　　2170

2171　　2172　　2173　　2174　　2175

2176-97. Wheel (*rimbo; Genji-guruma; kazaguruma; suisha*). Four types are included below: the Buddhist sacred wheel (*rimbo*, 2176–86), carriage wheel (*Genji-guruma*, 2187–93), pinwheel or wind wheel (*kazaguruma*, 2194–95), and waterwheel (*suisha*, 2196–97).

The sacred wheel, originally a weapon in ancient India, with swords as spokes, was adopted by esoteric Buddhism and used in ceremonies such as the taking of vows. Saicho and Kukai, founders of the Tendai and Shingon sects respectively, are said to have brought the implement to Japan. It symbolized both the wheel of the Law, and smoothing the path before one, or breaking down the enemies in one's own mind. To warriors, it also represented the cutting down of earthly foes, and as such was often used with the sword-blade device as a personal crest. The sacred wheel was by far the most widely adopted crest of Buddhist significance.

The wheel of the ox-drawn carriage takes its name from the Heian-period classic, *The Tale of Genji*. The elegant pattern depicting the wheel was popular in the latter half of that period, and shows the influence of the *Yamato-e* school of painting.

The waterwheel and pinwheel were not widespread motifs. The former appears to have been frequently mistakenly identified with the mallet motif and assumed some of the latter's auspicious connotations.

2198-2200. Wine Cup (*sakazuki*). Although saké had religious and ceremonial connotations from early times in Japan, the delicate saké cup was introduced as a design motif only in the late feudal period, when it carried a sense both of the pleasure quarters and of exchanging a pledge or promise.

2176 2177 2178 2179 2180
2181 2182 2183 2184 2185
2186 2187 2188 2189 2190
2191 2192 2193 2194 2195
2196 2197 2198 2199 2200

Patterns and Designs

2201-30. Circle: Enclosure (*wa*). As a crest by itself, the circle carries obvious connotations of perfection, harmony, completeness, integrity, even peace. In Japanese heraldry, the dominant use of the circle was not by itself, however, but as an enclosure for other motifs. This was a gradual development. At the beginning of the period of feudal strife, only a very small percentage (1/17 by one estimate) of emblems and crests had any sort of enclosure. By the end of the Edo period, approximately one-third of all formal family crests were enclosed, usually by a circular device. The enclosure served two purposes:

to make one's mark more distinctive; and to make possible subtle variations of crests among branches of the same family line. The introduction of more elaborate enclosures such as the chrysanthemum and wisteria rings did not occur until around the fourteenth century.

Ordinary circles are labeled according to their thickness, with terminology ranging from hairline to "snake's eye" (2206; cf. 2276–87). Following the double and triple rings, the enclosures below are "hazy plum blossom" (2208); "hazy circle" (2209); *suhama* (2210; cf. 2288–2300); moon (2211); snow (2212–13);

plum blossom (2214); chrysanthemum (2215–16); chrysanthemum leaf (2217); wisteria (2218–19); bamboo (2220–21); carriage wheel (2222); "melon" (2223–24; cf. 2401–25); metal handle (2225–26; cf. 1776–95); and arabesque (2229–30).

As the contents of other sections in this work reveal, an extremely large number of other subjects—bamboo leaves, pine trees and pine needles, rice plants, water plantain, palm fronds, well cribs, clouds, and fans, to mention but a few—can also be used to make enclosures for other motifs.

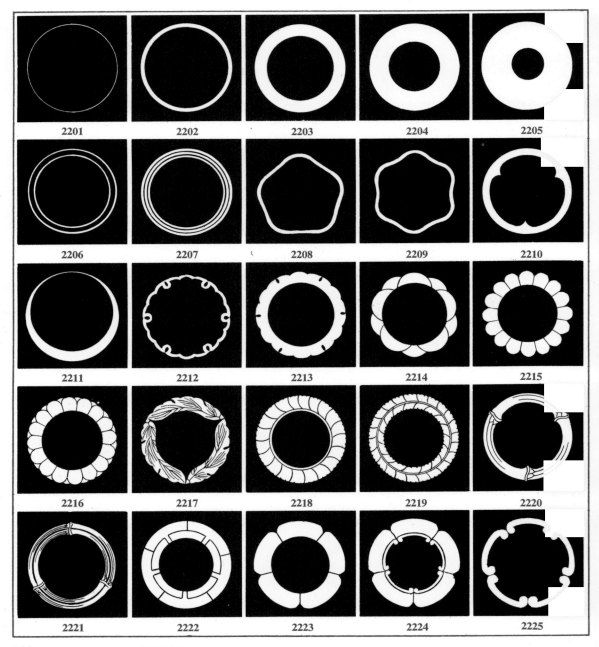

2231-35. Circle: Ball Rack (*mari-hasami*). Allegedly the stand in which a "kickball" was placed to keep it from rolling away (2235), the design probably preceded the label.

2236-50. Circle: Interlocked Rings (*kanawa; wachigai*). This motif is alleged to have been abstracted from a larger overall design in a manner similar to that in which the "seven treasures" motif, which follows, originated. For a similar motif, compare 1776–95.

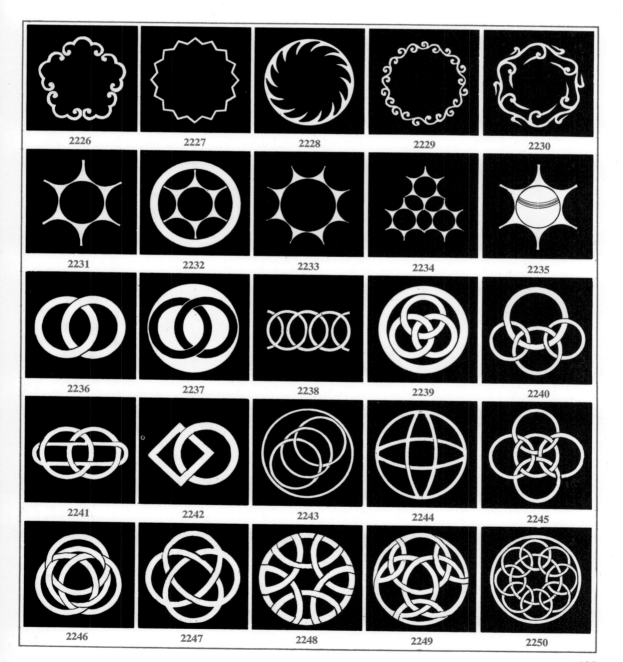

2226	2227	2228	2229	2230
2231	2232	2233	2234	2235
2236	2237	2238	2239	2240
2241	2242	2243	2244	2245
2246	2247	2248	2249	2250

2251-75. Circle: "Seven Treasures" (*shippo*). The *shippo* design appeared in the late Heian period as an abstraction from a large overall pattern of overlapping circles, the overlap being exactly equal on all four sides. Its name appears to derive from one of the inimitable Japanese puns, this one on *shi-ho*, or "four directions." The seven treasures are gold, silver, crystal, coral, agate, pearl, and lapis lazuli.

2276-87. Circle: "Snake's Eye" (*janome*). This motif was originally called *tsurumaki*, or "bowstring spool," because of its resemblance to the device on which warriors wound

their bowstring when the bow was unstrung. The spool was generally hung from the warrior's waist or from his large sword by a loop run through the hole in the spool center.

2288-2300. Circle: Suhama (*suhama*). A fashionable pattern in the Heian period, the curious *suhama* shape became one of the more popular motifs among family crests in the later feudal period. Supposedly suggestive of a beach or sandbar, the shape was primarily associated with small tray landscapes popular from the Heian period until recent times. Generally, the tray depicted a small seascape and was populated

with a crane, tortoise, pine, bamboo, and plum tree—the most auspicious of symbols. Occasionally the figures of an old man and woman were added, and in time the *suhama* shape itself absorbed the magic of its residents and became regarded as a lucky sign—particularly as a sign of longevity. This was reflected in one of its alternate names, *Horaidai*, or "Horai tray," for Horai was the name of a mythical island where people never died. In later centuries a certain kind of rice cake assumed both the name and shape of the *suhama*, but this was offspring and not parent of the traditional design.

2251	2252	2253	2254	2255
2256	2257	2258	2259	2260
2261	2262	2263	2264	2265
2266	2267	2268	2269	2270
2271	2272	2273	2274	2275

2276 2277 2278 2279 2280

2281 2282 2283 2284 2285

2286 2287 2288 2289 2290

2291 2292 2293 2294 2295

2296 2297 2298 2299 2300

2301-30. Diamond: Plain (*hishi*). The diamond or lozenge was a basic textile pattern in Japan from before the Heian period, having been originally brought to the islands from China. Its Japanese name is based on its resemblance to the leaf of the *hishi,* or water chestnut, and members of both the court and warrior societies used this as a favorite decoration even before the adoption of formal family crests. The vogue did not diminish, and by overlaying diamonds of various sizes, the range of variation was greatly increased.

2331-50. Diamond: Flower Diamond (*hanabishi*). Alongside the diamond, one of the earliest known textile patterns in Japan was the *karabana,* or "China flower," which follows below, and the natural melding of the two produced the four-petaled "flower diamond." The alternative name of this motif, *karabanabishi,* makes the combination explicit. The diamond category overall was one of the most popular of Japanese heraldic motifs.

2301 2302 2303 2304 2305
2306 2307 2308 2309 2310
2311 2312 2313 2314 2315
2316 2317 2318 2319 2320
2321 2322 2323 2324 2325

2326	2327	2328	2329	2330
2331	2332	2333	2334	2335
2336	2337	2338	2339	2340
2341	2342	2343	2344	2345
2346	2347	2348	2349	2350

2351-65. Flower: "China Flower" (*karabana*). *Kara,* usually translated simply as "China," is actually written with the ideograph for the T'ang dynasty, and the *kara*-flower is an almost archetypical example of the influence of T'ang even upon the fabrics worn by Japanese during this period. A purely Chinese design, not based on any one flower in particular, the *karabana* was popular in Japan at least from the Nara period, and is found as a decoration on many of the objects in the eighth-century imperial storehouse, the Shoso-in. As the continental design par excellence, it conveyed a particular sense

of elegance, and in later centuries a number of the members of the court (as opposed to warrior) aristocracy used this as a family emblem. The number of petals in the China-flower design varies, but is usually five. As such, the design bears a particularly close resemblance to the cherry blossom, the major difference between the two designs being in the treatment of the petal tips.

2365-70. Flower: "Brocade Flower" (*fusenryo*). Literally "floating-line weave," the *fusenryo* was originally a technical name for a kind of twill or brocade-weaving technique popular in the Heian period.

Eventually the name became applied to the type of complex circular floral pattern shown below.

2371-2400. Hexagon (*kikko*). The hexagon or carapace motif is a typical example of a pattern first popular among the courtly society as a decoration on clothing, furnishings, carriages, and the like, and later adopted as a formal heraldic emblem. *Kikko* literally means "tortoise shell," and this association imparted auspicious connotations to the hexagon. In addition, the carapace was the official emblem of the immensely influential Izumo Shrine, possibly because the tortoise is associated with

the god of the north, and Izumo is located in the northern part of Japan. Parishioners of Izumo and its associated shrines frequently adopted the hexagon as their own family crest to commemorate their devotion.

2376 2377 2378 2379 2380

2381 2382 2383 2384 2385

2386 2387 2388 2389 2390

2391 2392 2393 2394 2395

2396 2397 2398 2399 2400

2401-25. "Melon" (*mokko*). The nomenclature of this extremely popular and ancient design presents an etymological thicket. The pattern is known to have been used on court costumes in T'ang China. It was actually brought to Japan in the latter part of the sixth century, that is, before T'ang, and immediately assumed an honored place among the patterns used on Japanese court costumes. The original name probably derived from a decorated cloth screen (*misu no mokko*) placed around the seat of eminent persons to shield them from the gaze of lesser mortals. From this cloth, the label *mokko* was abstracted and applied to the pattern itself, and in later centuries the original derivation was forgotten and the ideographs for another *mokko,* meaning "melon," were applied to the same pattern. The cucumber is also included within the general category of melon in Japan, and it is assumed that the pattern was given this new label because it bears some resemblance to the cross section of a cucumber. The Oriental genius for linguistic obfuscation is carried a bit further in the case of the courtly-curtain-cucumber, for it is also sometimes labeled *ka,* meaning "nest," because of its alleged resemblance to the circular placement of eggs in their nests by such birds as the skylark. Well over 150 families ignored these problems and adopted the *mokko* as a family crest. Most often, the emblem enclosed some version of the "China flower."

2426-50. Square: Enclosure (*kaku*). The square or rectilinear perimeter is rarely used as a heraldic device by itself, but is frequently used as an enclosure for other motifs in the same manner as the circular enclosure. In addition to the shapes shown below, other motifs such as the well crib and diamond are also commonly used as rectilinear enclosures.

2401 2402 2403 2404 2405
2406 2407 2408 2409 2410
2411 2412 2413 2414 2415
2416 2417 2418 2419 2420
2421 2422 2423 2424 2425

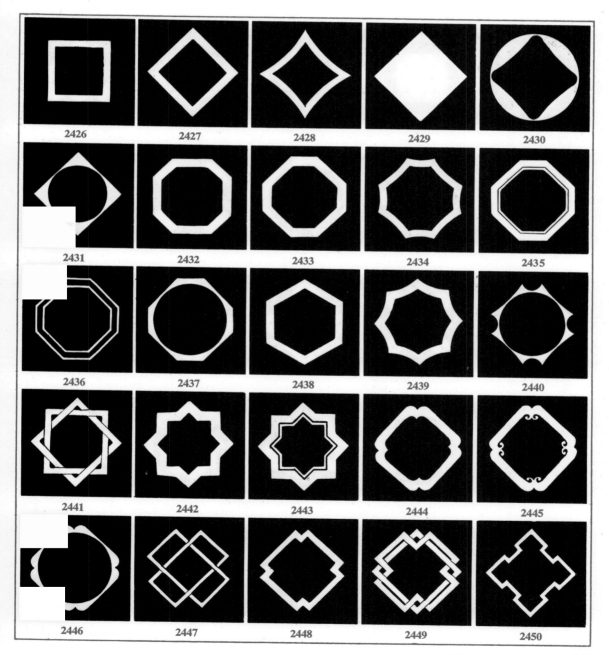

2426 2427 2428 2429 2430

2431 2432 2433 2434 2435

2436 2437 2438 2439 2440

2441 2442 2443 2444 2445

2446 2447 2448 2449 2450

2451-70. Square: "Mesh" (*meyui*). The ideographs with which this ancient pattern is described literally mean "eye tie," in reference to an expensive dyeing process in which the material is puckered and tied before coloring, to produce a dappled effect.

2471-82. Square: "Nail Extractor" (*kuginuki*). The simple small square in a large square offers one of the least simple nomenclatures and most outlandish puns in Japanese heraldry. The name apparently derived from the tip of a crowbar-like tool used by carpenters in premodern times. The nail is possibly suggested in several of the crests below (2473,

2477–79), and in one the old extractors are set against their modern counterpart (2472). This was one of the more popular motifs among the crests of high-ranking warrior families, partly because of its simplicity, but primarily because of its martial connotations. The very nature of the tool and its label conveyed a sense of great power from small origins, and this social application of the principle of leverage was reflected in one of the crest's alternative names, *manryoku,* "thousandfold power." That this meant more than court politics was reflected in a pun whereby the crest was identified with

four ideographs reading *ku-ki nuki* and meaning "pull up nine castles."

2483-2500. Square: "Paving Stone" (*ishidatami*). Among the rigidly prescribed court costumes of prefeudal Japan, the check pattern was so esteemed that its use was restricted to courtiers who ranked higher than the third rank. The "paving stone" motif reflects this esteem, rather than any particular significance attached to such stones themselves.

2476 2477 2478 2479 2480

2481 2482 2483 2484 2485

2486 2487 2488 2489 2490

2491 2492 2493 2494 2495

2496 2497 2498 2499 2500

2501-15. Stripe (*hikiryo*). In wartime, Japanese generals of the feudal period surrounded their encampments with huge cloth curtains. Usually these were made of several long strips of cloth sewn together horizontally and varying in color (usually white, blue, and black) to distinguish the individual general and his followers. The stripe thus assumed strong martial connotations, and became a mark of identification on personal military gear as well. In the early fourteenth century the heads of the Ashikaga and Nitta, then the two most powerful clans in Japan, both adopted stripe patterns as a family crest.

2516-20. Stripe: Divining Rod (*sangi*). Straight and square-cut stripes, usually numbering one to three, are associated both with an early method of divination and an early method by which mathematical calculations were made before invention of the abacus. In *sangi* divination, six square sticks with all four sides differently marked were used to tell fortunes. In *sangi* calculation, several hundred short sticks colored either black or red were laid out in a prescribed manner and used to perform either addition or subtraction.

Several unusual denotative crests were based on the *sangi*. The Miki family, whose surname is written with the characters for "three wood," used the three stripes and gained the added connotations of auspicious augury. More subtly, the Goto ("five wisteria") family used a crest composed of a wisteria ring with a single horizontal stripe, because in *sangi* calculation, one horizontally placed stick is equal to five units.

2521-22. Stripe: Offering (*oshiki ni san monji*). The *oshiki* is an old-style wooden container, usually made of cypress, used for food and associated primarily with offerings to the deities —an association similar to that of the urn. Some fifteen or twenty high-

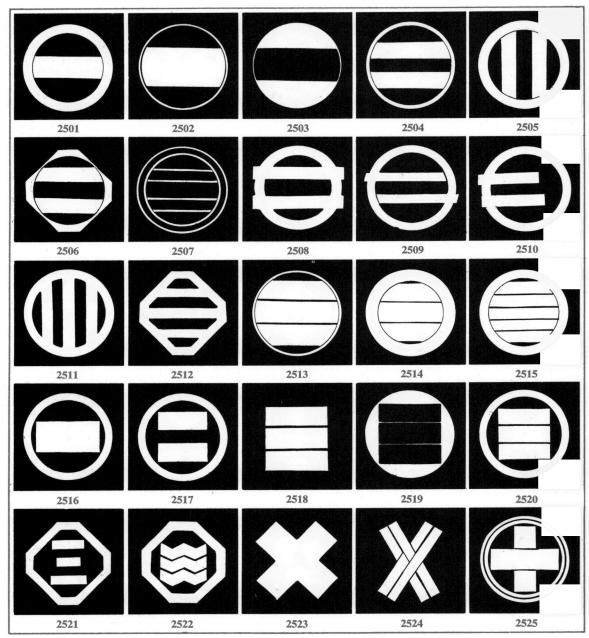

2501 2502 2503 2504 2505

2506 2507 2508 2509 2510

2511 2512 2513 2514 2515

2516 2517 2518 2519 2520

2521 2522 2523 2524 2525

ranking warrior families used it as a crest enclosure, with variations on three stripes inside. The latter actually represent the ideograph for "three" and commemorate devotion to the Mishima Shrine in Shikoku—the *mi* of Mishima also being written with the ideograph for the number three.

2523-30. Stripe: Diagonals (*sujikai; sujichigai; hikichigai*). The diagonal cross is an archetypical mark found in all primitive societies. In Japan, the design was also identified as wood or lumber (*ki*) or "crossed sticks" (*chigaibo*), and developed to include lattices and wattles.

2531-65. Tomoe. The original source and meaning of the *tomoe* design are a matter of some controversy. Yorisuke Numata, Japan's foremost authority on heraldic design, maintained that the basic "comma" shape emerged independently as a design in Japan, being a picture (*e*) of a leather guard worn on the left wrist by archers to receive the impact of the bowstring after it had been released; the guard was called a *tomo,* and the design a *tomo*-picture, or *tomo-e*. Other commentators point to the existence of a similar pattern throughout the world, citing its appearance on artifacts in ancient

China and Korea, among both the Basques in Spain and certain tribes in Siberia, and as a quasi-religious symbol in ancient Greece and Egypt. They stress its resemblance to the comma-shaped *magatama* jewels found in prehistoric tomb sites in Japan, and one persuasive argument traces the *tomoe* back to ancient Chinese depictions of the snake. The latter interpretation relates directly to primitive religious belief in the snake as a symbol of the *yin-yang* cosmology.

The commentators do agree upon a somewhat surprising fact: that the *tomoe* pattern was not one of the

basic elements of early Japanese design, and in fact did not become fashionable until around the tenth or eleventh century. Although a *tomoe* pattern dating back to the mid-Nara period was recently discovered, the design is conspicuously absent from the major collection of treasures from this period stored in the Shoso-in. Once introduced, however, the popularity of the design was immediate and immense, and by the end of the feudal period the *tomoe* ranked second only to the paulownia as a favorite motif for family crests.

Whatever the original meaning of the *tomoe* may have been, in Japan it assumed an essentially independent existence. In the late Heian period, the *tomoe* became by far the most popular decoration under the eaves and on the tiled roof edges of temples—apparently in the belief that the design represented a whirlpool and would serve the talismanic purpose of waterproofing the building. Thus, simultaneous with its emergence as a popular personal ornament, the *tomoe* acquired a general religious connotation. In the period of feudal strife, this became more specific as the *tomoe* came to be regarded as the personal symbol of Hachiman, god of war. As a heraldic device, the *tomoe* was thus not merely an elegant and dynamic design in its own right, but also possessed desirable religious and martial qualities. The last three crests are based on the ideograph for *tomoe*.

2566-75. Triangle (*uroko*). The triangle as a crest developed from an ancient textile pattern. As a heraldic device it assumed a new label—*uroko* or "fish scale"—and its most illustrious association was with the powerful Hojo family, who ruled Japan for almost a century and a half at the beginning of the feudal period.

2551	2552	2553	2554	2555
2556	2557	2558	2559	2560
2561	2562	2563	2564	2565
2566	2567	2568	2569	2570
2571	2572	2573	2574	2575

Symbols and Ideographs

2576-85. Buddhist Swastika (*man-ji*). The swastika symbol is found among the primitive cultures of such distant countries as Babylon, Assyria, Italy, Greece, Hungary, England, Mexico, and Peru. It was transmitted to Japan from India through China, and associated from the start there with Buddhism. Although widely displayed, particularly on Buddhist temple architecture, the swastika does not appear to have borne a heavy burden of symbolism in Japan. Rather, it was interpreted primarily as good luck, and was even sometimes used as a hidden cross.

2586-95. Cross (*kurusu*). In the century following Francis Xavier's arrival in Japan in 1549, the number of Japanese converts to Christianity is estimated to have reached close to half a million. Most of these resided in west and southwest Japan, and a number were of high rank, including several daimyo families. The cross was publicly displayed, and a number of Christian warriors adopted it as a personal crest to be placed on their battle gear and banners. The renowned Konishi Yukinaga led a predominantly Christian army beneath banners marked with the cross during the ill-considered Japanese invasions

of Korea in 1592 and 1597, for example, and a number of the warriors who unsuccessfully defended Osaka Castle against Tokugawa Ieyasu in 1615 were converts who inscribed Christian insignia on their flags. As described by C. R. Boxer, Padre João Rodriguez Girão recorded that at this latter battle "there were so many crosses, Jesus, and Santiagos on the flags, tents, and other martial insignia which the Japanese used in their encampments, that this must needs have made Ieyasu sick to his stomach." Even this, however, was not the high point of the display of Christian emblems in Japan. In the

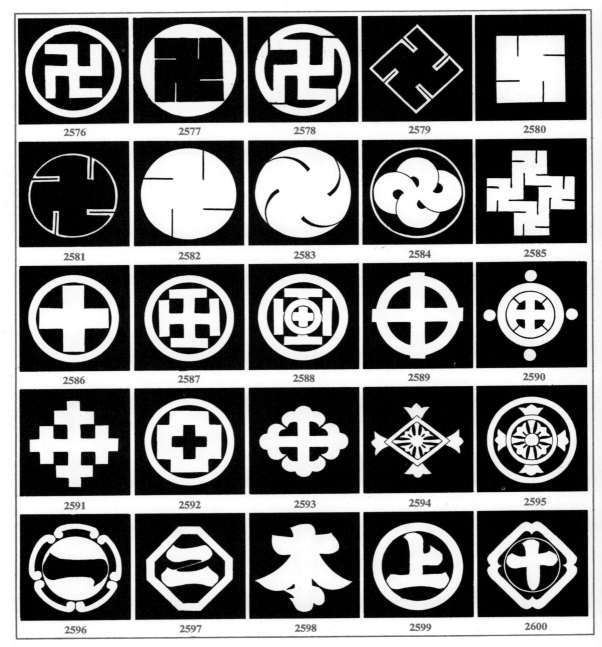

celebrated Christian-led uprising at Shimabara from 1637 to 1638, some thirty thousand men, women, and children fought beneath almost exclusively Christian banners, some inscribed in Portuguese, until they were massacred with but a single reputed survivor. When Christianity was banned in the 1630's, these symbols were proscribed and many secret believers then resorted to the "hidden cross" visible in such traditional crest motifs as the amulet, horse's bit, crossed oars, and the like.

2596-2670. Ideographs (*ji*). Characters or ideographs were used as crests for any number of reasons, the most common being auspicious or denotative. Auspicious ideographs included those meaning "great," "above," "good luck," "profit," "fortune," "longevity," "increase," "myriad," and so on. Denotative ideograph crests were those which included one character of the family's name.

Some ideograph crests had special religious significance, such as the character for "existence," which was associated with the Izumo Shrine, and *mu* (nothingness; void), which reflected the teachings of Zen Buddhism. Also involving religious connotations were many ideographs for numbers, such as three, associated with the Oyamazumi Shrine; and eight (*hachi*), which is the first character of the name of Hachiman, god of war. The character for the number nine was adopted as a crest by several families because it was the number assigned to *yang*, the dynamic, masculine force of the cosmic *yin-yang* dualism, and several families used a plaque with the ideographs for twenty-eight written on it, a reference to the twenty-eight parts into which ancient geomancers divided the celestial sphere.

As the selection below indicates, ideographs were subject to depiction

in a wide variety of styles, from the orthodox brush stroke to the geometric rendition to the fully abstract. Almost any ideograph can be read with several different pronunciations, with the context and convention determining which of these is appropriate. The printed form of each ideograph presented below, together with its most common reading and English translation, is provided in the appendix on page 155.

2671. Pentagram (*Abe Seimei han*). In Japan, the pentagram was a talisman used in *yin-yang* geomancy. Its name, meaning "the seal of Abe Seimei," refers to the foremost geo-mancer in Japanese history, who lived in the mid-Heian period. The symbol is still used today on the swaddling clothes of newborn infants in Japan.

2672. Symbol of the Absolute (*tai-kyoku-zu*). The symbol of the Absolute, which clearly reflects the *yin-yang* dualism, actually was devised during the Sung dynasty in China (960–1126) under the primary influence of Neo-Confucianism, and became well known in Japan only during the Confucian revival of the Edo period.

2673-74. Symbols of Perfection and Heaven and Earth (*enso; tenchi*). In the symbol of divination, the circle by itself is perfection, harmony. The circle and square together are heaven and earth, the universe.

2675. Yin-Yang Symbol (*inyo-zu*). The dualism of the universe—passive-active, dark-light, female-male—is juxtaposed in the basic symbol of the *yin-yang* cosmology. In ancient Chinese thought, the interaction of these two cosmic forces, complementary but unequal, produced the Five Elements and from these in turn the multiplicity of the universe.

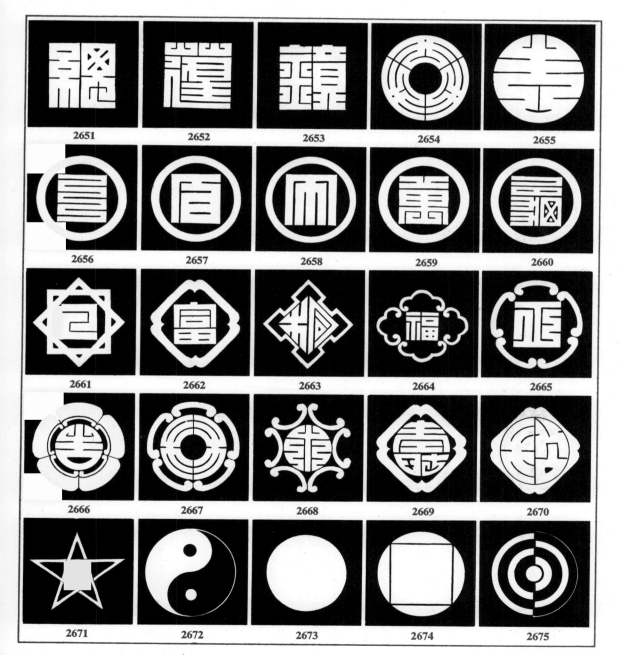

2651   2652   2653   2654   2655

2656   2657   2658   2659   2660

2661   2662   2663   2664   2665

2666   2667   2668   2669   2670

2671   2672   2673   2674   2675

2676-2715. Incense Symbols (*Genji ko-zu*). The art of mixing and judging perfumes is known to have existed in Japan as early as the sixth century. By the ninth century, perfumes were one of the chief imports in the luxury trade with China, and by the late tenth century the art was so highly refined and esteemed in Heian society that two of the main characters in *The Tale of Genji* are named (as Ivan Morris renders them) Lord Fragrance and Prince Scent. In Genji's patrician world, perfume was a manly concern (partly because people bathed infrequently), and the blending of scents and incense developed to the point where different schools emerged, each with its own conventions. "Scent contests" (*koawase*) remained popular even after the decline of the courtly class, and by the early Edo period were fashionable among virtually all strata of society. Despite prohibitive sumptuary legislation, the practice survived, and in fact it appears to have been during the Edo period that the "Genji incense symbols" depicted below first appeared.

The Genji incense symbols were originally associated with one particular type of incense ceremony, in which five different primary scents were used, each being divided into five packets. Each of the resulting twenty-five packets was differently marked with a symbol such as those depicted below. Various combinations selected from among the packets were then mixed and burned. In time the number of symbols was expanded to fifty-four, corresponding to the number of chapters in *The Tale of Genji*. Each was associated with a specific chapter, and eventually set pictorial designs correlated to both the symbols and the narrative were created.

In the Edo period, several families particularly infatuated with the art of perfumes used these as crests.

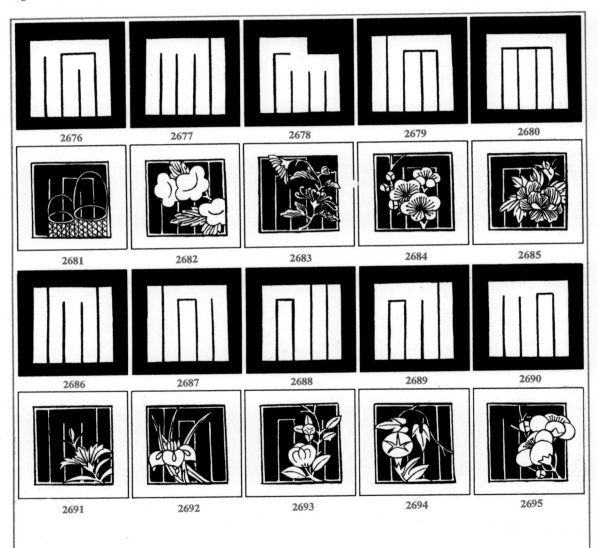

2676   2677   2678   2679   2680

2681   2682   2683   2684   2685

2686   2687   2688   2689   2690

2691   2692   2693   2694   2695

In the arrangement given below, incense symbols have been placed above the appropriate pictorial designs to show the graphic relationships.

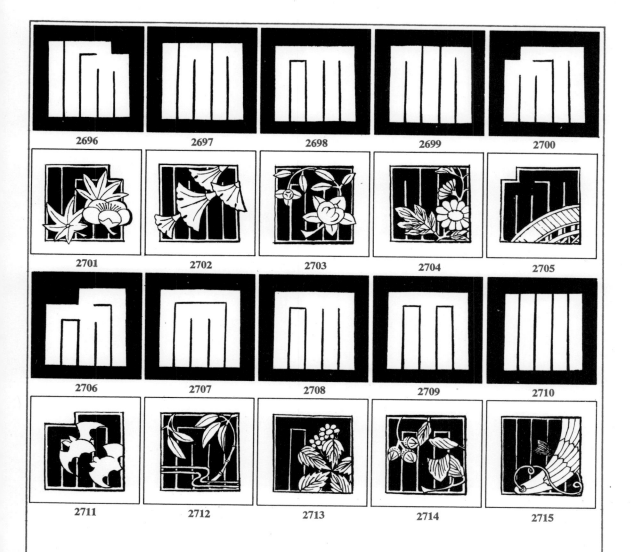

2696 2697 2698 2699 2700

2701 2702 2703 2704 2705

2706 2707 2708 2709 2710

2711 2712 2713 2714 2715

Appendix: Common Readings
of Ideograph Crests
(2596-2670)

NOTE: Readings given in roman typeface are usually independent words; those in italic typeface are used when the character appears in a compound. Numbers in parentheses refer to the number of times the ideograph appears in the crest.

CREST NO.	IDEO-GRAPH	READING	MEANING
2596	一	ichi	one
2597	二	ni	two
2598	本	moto	origin; foundation
2599	上	ue	up; above
2600	十	*jū*	ten
2601	平	taira	equality; peace
2602	利	*ri*	profit
2603	千	sen	one thousand
2604	志	kokoro-zashi	will; determination
2605	萬	*man*	ten thousand
2606	千切	chigiri	(cf. 2062–75)
2607	歳	toshi	age; year
2608	正	*shō*	correct; righteousness
2609	圓	*en*	circle; perfection
2610	亀	kame	tortoise
2611	宝	takara	treasure
2612	福	*fuku*	good fortune
2613	壽	kotobuki	congratulation; longevity
2614	鶴	tsuru	crane
2615	巴	tomoe	tomoe (3)
2616	かゞ	kaga	Kaga (surname) (8)
2617	竹	take	bamboo
2618	魚	sakana	fish

CREST NO.	IDEO-GRAPH	READING	MEANING
2619	叶	kanau	grant wish
2620	主	*shu*	lord; master
2621	木	ki	tree
2622	吉	*kichi*	luck; joy
2623	川	kawa	river
2624	天	*ten*	heaven
2625	品	shina	quality
2626	中	naka	center (3)
2627	小	*sho*	small
2628	十	*jū*	ten
2629	十	*jū*	ten
2630	大	*dai*	great
2631	大	*dai*	great (3)
2632	中	naka	center
2633	吉	*kichi*	luck; joy (3)
2634	戸	*to*	door
2635	壽	kotobuki	congratulation; longevity
2636	泰	*tai*	security
2637	礼	*rei*	propriety
2638	倹	*ken*	frugality
2639	仁	*jin*	benevolence
2640	知	*chi*	knowledge
2641	温	*on*	warmth
2642	良	*ryō*	good

CREST NO.	IDEO-GRAPH	READING	MEANING
2643	信	*shin*	sincerity
2644	義	*gi*	integrity
2645	讓	*jō*	bequeath
2646	貞	*tei*	chastity
2647	德	*toku*	virtue
2648	雁	kari	wild goose
2649	量	*ryō*	quantity
2650	糠	nuka	rice bran
2651	總	*sō*	all
2652	蓬	yomogi	mugwort
2653	鏡	kagami	mirror
2654	西	nishi	west (3)
2655	吉	*kichi*	luck, joy
2656	一	ichi	one
2657	百	*hyaku*	one hundred

CREST NO.	IDEO-GRAPH	READING	MEANING
2658	千	sen	one thousand
2659	萬	*man*	ten thousand
2660	亀	kame	tortoise
2661	巴	tomoe	tomoe
2662	富	tomi	wealth
2663	桐	kiri	paulownia
2664	福	*fuku*	good fortune
2665	正	*shō*	correct; righteousness
2666	吉	*kichi*	luck; joy
2667	森	mori	grove
2668	木	ki	tree
2669	壽	kotobuki	congratulation; longevity
2670	松	matsu	pine

Bibliographic Notes

T HE BASIC RESEARCH concerning the history and significance of Japanese crests was done several decades ago by Yorisuke Numata. His encyclopedic volume entitled *Nihon Monshogaku* (Japanese Heraldry), first published in 1925, draws upon a broad range of classical Japanese sources and remains the basis of most contemporary accounts dealing with this subject. The present work is no exception: *Nihon Monshogaku* is the single most important reference used in preparing both the introduction and the commentaries of *The Elements of Japanese Design*. Several shorter books by Mr. Numata are also useful. *Nihon Monshogaku: Koyo* (Japanese Heraldry: Outline), 1937 an abbreviated version of the above text, cuts closer to the bones of the subject and conveniently presents in the form of charts some of the data that appeared as textual description in the longer work. *Monsho Sowa* (Anecdotes about Crests), 1935, focuses on the more lively aspects of the subject, and *Monsho no Kenkyu* (The Study of Crests), 1941, provides an insight into heraldic research in a Japanese setting.

A number of more recent Japanese books are also useful as reference sources. *Nihon no Kamon* (Family Crests of Japan), 1964, by Shinshi Yoshimoto and Hideyuki Kato covers the same ground as Numata, although with less depth and authority. *Nihon no Monsho* (Crests of Japan), 1965, by Kosaku Ito is a well-produced collection of over four thousand crests with concise and useful running commentaries accompanying each motif. This work also includes photographs depicting the various items on which crests were displayed, but in this respect falls far behind the handsome two-volume edition subsequently prepared by the same author and produced by Bijutsu Shuppan-sha under the title *Monsho* (Crests), 1969.

Among the many attractive *moncho,* or catalogues of crests, which still are to be found in Japanese libraries and secondhand bookstores, two of fairly recent origin might be singled out here. *Monten* (Book of Crests), edited by Jiichiro Ichida, was originally published in 1932 and more recently reprinted in 1956; this is a fairly comprehensive collection of approximately forty-six hundred crests—including separate sections for the emblems of towns and cities, actors, shrines and temples, and the like—and includes a clear, printed identification of the technical name of each individual crest. *Heian Monkan* (Heian Mirror of Crests), compiled by Enosuke Inuke in 1936, is one of the most beautifully printed and bound of the later crest catalogues and particularly interesting because of its inclusion of samples of such dandified crests as the *datemon.*

A useful source for identifying the genealogical associations of specific crests (a thicket not entered in the present work) is the *Daibukan* (Great Book of Heraldry) edited by Hiroshi Hashimoto and reprinted in a six-volume revised edition in 1940; this is a collection of fifty Edo-period books of heraldry (*bukan*) and contains, in addition to line drawings of family crests, a variety of miscellaneous information about members of the ruling warrior class. Illustrated critiques (*hyobanki*) of the courtesans and actors of the Edo period can be found most conveniently in the extensive series of facsimiles identified as *Kisho Fuku-*

sei Kai (Reproductions of Rare Books); published between 1918 and 1942, this consists of reproductions of 468 different popular works depicting the life of the demimonde and incidentally revealing the fashionable use to which crests were put during this period. *Shikido Okagami* (Great Mirror of the Way of Love), a late-seventeenth-century description of the licensed quarters which contains a separate section on courtesans' crests, is available in a 1961 reproduction. One of the most comprehensive and useful single articles dealing with the actors' critiques of the Edo period is by Tatsuyuki Takano and appears in both *Kokugekishi Gaikan* (An Outline of the History of Native Theater), 1934, and, in slightly less complete form, as an entry in *Engekishi Kenkyu* (Studies on the History of the Theater), 1932, I: 223–92. An account of the firefighters of Edo and their "heraldic" paraphernalia can be found in *Nihon Fuzoku Shi* (History of Japanese Customs), VII: 173–210.

A variety of general Japanese reference works were also consulted in preparing the present book, among them the familiar *Kojien* and such encyclopedias as the *Daihyakka Jiten, Engeki Hyakka Daijiten, Nihon Bungaku Daijiten, Nihon Shakai Minzoku Jiten*, and *Sekai Daihyakka Jiten.*

In English, a convenient small volume by Yuzuru Okada, *Japanese Family Crests,* was published by the Japanese government in 1941. The symbols of the early Japanese emperors are discussed by W. G. Aston and precisely illustrated in the 1894 issue of *Transactions of the Asiatic Society of Japan,* XXII: 1, and one of the earliest attempts to deal with Japanese crests in English was published by Thomas R. H. McClatchie as early as 1877 in the same journal, V: 1. Articles by Gordon Ambrose Lee and A. J. Koop pick up the topic of Japanese crests in the 1909 and 1911 volumes of *Transactions and Proceedings of the Japan Society,* London, VIII and IX. A German study of Japanese heraldry which identifies the crests used by leading daimyo families and is illustrated with excellent engravings was published in Vienna in 1906 by Hugo Gerard Ströl under the title *Japanisches Wappenbuch.*

Literary writings are a primary source of information concerning both Japanese crests and the larger dimension of Oriental symbolism, and several English translations of Japanese classics have been particularly helpful in preparing the present work. The greatest of the war chronicles, *Heike Monogatari,* appears in a vivid (although sometimes erroneous) translation by A. L. Sadler in the 1918 and 1921 issues of *Transactions of the Asiatic Society of Japan,* XLVI: 2 and XLIX: 1; this deals with the Gempei War of 1180–85 and contains numerous episodes revealing the first tentative gestures toward the use of crests as a mark of personal identification on the battlefield. The full flower of Japanese heraldry among the warrior class is conveyed in the *Taiheiki,* available in a careful partial translation by Helen Craig McCullough (1959); Mrs. McCullough's introduction provides a good insight into the manner in which war was waged in feudal Japan. The dandification of crests in the ebullient popular culture of the early Edo period is best revealed in the writings of Saikaku; in particular see *The Japanese Family Storehouse* (1959), translated by G. W. Sargent, and *The Floating World in Japanese Fiction* (1959) by Howard Hibbett.

Several sources provide insight into the lives of the courtesans. Donald H. Shively offers perhaps the best study of the subject in the introduction to his translation of Chikamatsu, *The Love Suicide at Amijima* (1953). A fascinating and neglected first-hand account of the Yoshiwara quarter by J. E. DeBecker was published in London in 1899 under the title *The Nightless City.* Insight into the early history of the Kabuki theater is provided in works by Faubion Bowers, Earle Ernst, and Zoë Kincaid. Reference has also been made to unpublished papers by Olof Lidin and P. Tsurumi on *hyobanki* and *bukan* respectively. On changing fashions in Japanese dress, see Helen Benton Minnich, *Japanese Costume and the Makers of Its Elegant Tradition* (1963).

For matters of general historical background, the standard references used were George Sansom's several volumes on premodern Japan, in addition to *East Asia: The Great Tradition* (1958) by Edwin O. Reischauer and John K. Fairbank. Sansom's urbane treatment of the culture and values of the Heian period is complemented by Ivan Morris's delineation of Heian life in *The World of the Shining Prince* (1964).

Index

Figures in italic typeface refer to pages on which the crest illustrations appear, those in roman typeface indicate text references.

daimyo, 9, 12, 18, 159
dances, 104–5, 106, 118
dandified crests, 21, 34, 157–58
"dandruff remover," 108
Danjūrō, *see* Ichikawa Danjūrō
Date family, 14
datemon, 21, 33
decapitation, 26, 63, 110, 120
decoration, 29, *109,* 116
deer, 26, 30, 88, *92*
demon, 32, 58, *92–93,* 98, 107; *see also* exorcism
denotative crests, 33–34, 42, 47, 55, 60, 62, 72, 77, 82, 90, 98, 99, 120, 124, 128, 144, 149
diagonal lines, 26, 30, 145
diamond, 7, 34, 54, 72, *136–37,* 140
divination, 32, 33, 144, 150; *see also sangi*
divining rod, *144*
doll, *109*
dragon, 3, 26, 31, 92, *93,* 116
dragonfly, 28, 29, *94*
drum, 34, *110*
dumpling, 26, *110*
"Dutch hat" crest, 24
dyeing, 15, 17, 23, 56, 74, 142

earth, 40–44, 150
eboshi, 114–15
Edo, 42-3
Edo Castle, 16
Edo period, 12, 13, 14, 15, 16–24, 32, 34, 40, 47, 80, 102–3, 104, 105, 106, 107, 108, 109, 110–11, 115, 116, 118, 127, 132, 150, 152, 157–58
eggplant, *56*
Egypt, 145
Eiga Monogatari scroll, 51
Eiraku tsuhō, 108
Eisai, Zen monk, 78
enclosures, 11, 15, 21, 40 (moon-cloud), 42 (snow), 53 (chrysanthemum), 72 (pine needle), 77 (rice plant), 128 (well crib), 132 (arabesque, bamboo, carriage wheel, chrysanthemum, chrysanthemum leaf, circle, handle, "hazy circle," "hazy plum blossom," "melon," moon, plum blossom, "snake's-eye," snow, *suhama*), 140 ("melon," square), 145 (stripe)
Engishiki, 97
England, 148
ensō, 150, *151*
eta class, 18
Europe, heraldry of compared to Japan, ix, 11, 13, 14, 15, 17, 18, 19, 25, 35
evil spirits, 29; *see also* demon; exorcism
exorcism, 29, 32, 33, 58, 60, 70, 98, 104, 107

"eyeball" crest, 23
"eye tie" dyeing, *142*

falcon, 28, 30, *94,* 105
family, 4, 6, 8, 9–10, 132
family crest, *see* formal crests; substitute crests
fan, 25, 27, 29, 34, 44, 66, *110–12,* 132
Faust, 33
feather, 7, 28, 30, *94*
feather duster, 112, *113*
feather fan, 111, *112*
fence, 30, 46, 112, *113*
fern, 29, *56*
fertility, 29, 40, 76, 84
festivals, 52 (Chrysanthemum), 58 (Bon), 58 (Hollyhock), 58 (Kamo Festival), 60 (Iris), 62 (Boys'), 62 (Girls'), 64 (Tanabata)
firearms, 11
fire bell, *105*
fire-fighting companies, 17, 105, 158
fish, 4, 10; "fish scale," 26, *146*
"five elements," 150
"five grains," 58, 63
"five virtues," 126
flag, 6, 7, 11, 16, 17, 27, 44, 112, *113*
flax, *see* hemp
"floating world," ix, 16–24, 115, 118
floral patterns, 8, 28, 34, 136–38; *see also under individual names*
"flower diamond," 136, *137*
foliage, 4; *see also* maple leaf; oak
formal crests, 4, 5, 7, 9, 10, 14–5, 16, 18, 23, 132, 157–58
forsythia, *56*
"four auspicious creatures," 93
"four directions," 134
"four great clans," 10
"four princes" of art, 52, 64
Fujiwara clan, 4, 10, 12, 33, 82
fukumon, 15
furoshiki, 120
Fusenchō, 27, 89
fusenryō, 138

gardenia, *56*
geisha, *see* courtesan
Gempei Seisuiki, 27
Gempei War, 6, 7, 25, 111–12, 158
genealogies, 10, 12, 14, 22, 34, 82, 157; *see also* books of heraldry
Genji, *see* Minamoto clan
Genji kō-zu, 152–53
Genji Monogatari, 118, 130, 152

The "weathermark" identifies this book as having been planned, designed, and produced at the Tokyo offices of John Weatherhill, Inc. / Book design and typography by Meredith Weatherby and Ronald Bell / Composition by General Printing Co., Yokohama / Platemaking and printing by Kinmei Printing Co., Tokyo / Bound at the Okamoto Binderies, Tokyo / The typeface used is Monotype Times New Roman, with hand-set Perpetua for display.

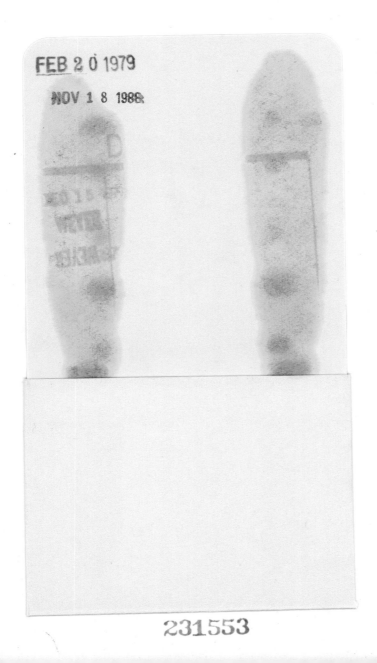